Every Day with Jesus

JAN/FEB 2017

Free to Live

**'Direct my footsteps according to your word;
let no sin rule over me.'** Psalm 119:133

Selwyn Hughes
Revised and updated by Mick Brooks

© CWR 2016. Dated text previously published as *Every Day with Jesus: Divine Mastery* (January/February 2003) by CWR. This edition revised and updated for 2017 by Mick Brooks.

CWR, Waverley Abbey House, Waverley Lane, Farnham, Surrey GU9 8EP, UK Tel: 01252 784700
Email: mail@cwr.org.uk Registered Charity No. 294387. Registered Limited Company No. 1990308.

Unless otherwise indicated, all Scripture references are from the Holy Bible: New International Version (NIV), Copyright © 1979, 1984 by Biblica (formerly International Bible Society). Used by permission of Hodder & Stoughton Publishers, an Hachette UK company. All rights reserved. 'NIV' is a registered trademark of Biblica (formerly International Bible Society). UK trademark number 1448790. Other versions used are marked: KJV: King James Version. Public Domain. TLB: The Living Bible copyright © 1971 by Tyndale House Foundation. Used by permission of Tyndale House Publishers Inc., Carol Stream, Illinois 60188. All rights reserved. *The Message*: THE MESSAGE. Copyright © 1993, 1994, 1995, 1996, 2000, 2001, 2002. Used by permission of NavPress Publishing Group.

Every effort has been made to ensure that these devotional notes contain the correct permissions, but if anything has been inadvertently overlooked the Publisher will be pleased to make the necessary arrangements at the first opportunity. Please contact the Publisher directly.

Cover image: Joel Bear Studios/Stocksy
Quiet Time image: pixabay/public domain pictures
Printed in England by Linney Print

Every Day with Jesus is available in large print from CWR. It is also available on **audio and DAISY** in the UK and Eire for the sole use of those with a visual impairment worse than N12, or who are registered blind. For details please contact **Torch Trust for the Blind**, Torch House, Torch Way, Northampton Road, Market Harborough LE16 9HL. Tel: 01858 438260.

A word of introduction...

After the past year in the UK, I cannot possibly fully know what 2017 holds – either nationally or personally. But what I do know to be true is that God is the same today as He was yesterday. He has promised to build His Church and nothing – nothing – can stand against it. I know He is a deeply personal Father and He is able to use setbacks as springboards and turns stumbling blocks into stepping stones.

In such changing times I find that all too frequently I can be overtaken by life. I can find myself constrained and constricted by circumstances – and expectations borne out of previous circumstances. In those moments, if we are not careful, we accept things as they are and our energy is put into keeping on going rather than exploring new ways of living. In this issue we begin to explore God's ways of living.

May this year be a time of walking every day with Jesus. He is our rearguard. We are not hemmed in, suppressed and suffocated by life circumstances; we are hemmed in by God who goes before us, guides and uphold us, and is always with us. So at the beginning of this new year, regardless of external circumstances and situations, I pray that you will find sacred spaces in this secular world, that God will direct your path and that you will discover freedom to live as He originally intended.

Mick Brooks, Consulting Editor

New year, new look!
We've freshened up the look of your *Every Day with Jesus* – hope you like it!

Free small group resources to accompany this issue can be found at **www.cwr.org.uk/extra**
The *EDWJ* Facebook community is growing! To join the conversation visit **www.facebook.com/edwjpage**

Turning the tables

FOR READING & MEDITATION – 1 CORINTHIANS 6:12–20

'"Everything is permissible for me"– but I will not be mastered by anything.' (v12)

We begin a new year by focusing on the theme of walking in freedom. It is a time to turn the tables on the things that are mastering us and, through the strength and grace that God gives us, learn to live life to the full. In the text before us today Paul tells us that he will not be mastered by anything. Rather, he has willingly given himself fully to the Master. In 2 Corinthians 5:14 he says, 'Christ's love compels us'. The word 'compels' could also be translated 'masters'. Paul was saying that his life goal was to not be mastered by anything other than Jesus.

Today's text can be seen as the greatest declaration of life purpose there has ever been. Those who have not given themselves to a relationship with Jesus will most likely be motivated and mastered by material things, circumstances, the world, disappointments and a whole host of other matters. As together we contemplate the year ahead, I cannot promise you a new set of circumstances or an easy path. Life is often difficult, and it is more than likely that this year will have its share of pain and disappointments. But, in the name of Him who sits on the throne, I *can* promise you that, as you seek to trust His Word and His truth then, like the apostle Paul, instead of being mastered by them you can walk in freedom.

God can break every shackle that binds us – whether it is the pull of our old nature or that of the devil himself. It's not a change in our external circumstances that we need – it's a change in ourselves. Self-mastery will not achieve this but giving ourselves in trust to God will. Make up your mind to submit to His loving care – beginning today.

FURTHER STUDY

Psa. 97:1–12;
Rom. 5:15–21

1. Over what does the Lord reign?

2. In what sphere are we, as believers, said to 'reign'?

God my Father, I realise that separated from You, I am easily mastered by all manner of things. With You, I am mastered by nothing – except You. I accept Your word to me today and begin the quest for freedom with eager anticipation. Amen.

The terrible twins

FOR READING & MEDITATION – PSALM 27:1–14

'The LORD is my light and my salvation – whom shall I fear?' (v1)

The freedom we are thinking about in these meditations is God-given, not self-mastery. Self-mastery will falter and eventually fail.

The will to live, and live *fully*, is a compelling motivation that drives us. And the drive for perfection is perhaps one of the most powerful motivations in creation, including the new creation. 'Religion,' said Dr E. Stanley Jones, 'is the life urge turned qualitative.' Once we come into relationship with Jesus we find that we *want* to live fuller and better lives. 'But the will to live,' said Stanley Jones, 'may turn into mere willpower unless it is harnessed by qualitative factors. The will to mastery may become the will to tyranny unless controlled by the will of God.'

Permit me to ask you: What controls or masters you? Is it fear and worry? Is it your own wants? Is it self-pity, disappointment, bitterness or maybe resentment? These things turn the will to live into the desire to withdraw from life. But take heart. As we give ourselves more fully to God, we learn that He is more than a match for every situation and circumstance.

Of the things that *can* control us, let's start by looking at fear and worry. Many are mastered by these terrible twins. 'Do not fret,' we are instructed in Psalm 37:8, 'it leads only to evil.' 'Fretting' is destructive, as what begins as a fret can soon become a threat – a threat to personal peace. When studying psychology, I heard a psychiatrist say, 'Fear and worry are the greatest duality of evils a person can take into his or her life.' Let's not provide any fertile soil for them to take root in.

FURTHER STUDY

Psa. 118:1–9;
Luke 1:68–75

1. In what ways does the psalmist deal with his own fear?

2. What do the blessings of salvation include, according to Zechariah?

Father, I do not want the weeds of fear, worry and anxiety to take root in my life. May I not be controlled by them, but by You. Help me to gain complete freedom from all paralysing inhibitions and fears. In Jesus' name. Amen.

FOR READING & MEDITATION – JOB 3:20–26

'What I feared has come upon me; what I dreaded has happened to me.' (v25)

Yesterday we said that fear and worry can be paralysing and need to be rooted out of our lives. Psychologists point out that there is a type of fear that can be beneficial. For example, a degree of fear may make surgeons more careful, but fear pushed past a certain point could inhibit – or even paralyse – them. Fear, therefore, can be healthy as well as unhealthy. 'The fear of the LORD,' Scripture tells us, 'is the beginning of wisdom' (Psa. 111:10). Elsewhere we read, 'I was afraid and went out and hid your talent in the ground' (Matt. 25:25). Both verses are profoundly true: there is a fear that leads to wisdom and there is a fear that leads to paralysis – the latter causes us to bury our talents. Fear, like any other emotion, can be understood, brought to God and used for constructive purposes.

A woman I knew was obsessed by her fear of bacteria. She became a prisoner of that fear and stayed inside her house, terrified of what might infect her if she stepped outside. I can tell you that the fear inside her soul was far more deadly than any bacteria. This is a fairly extreme example of paralysing fear, but we can all have certain fears that block faith and prevent us from following God wholeheartedly.

Listen again to what Job said: 'What I feared has come upon me; what I dreaded has happened to me.' That did not happen by chance; that was cause and effect. Job started, it seems, without any fear other than the fear of God, but an unhealthy fear appears to have set in by this point in his life. E. Stanley Jones said, 'Fear is sand in the machinery of life.' With God's help we should master fear before it masters us.

FURTHER STUDY

1 Kings 19:3–18; John 14:1–11

1. What helped Elijah overcome his fear?

2. How did Jesus reassure His disciples in a time of fear?

Father, You have fashioned me for faith, not fear. May I walk this day and every day in confident faith, afraid of nothing. In Jesus' name. Amen.

Worry – a form of atheism

FOR READING & MEDITATION – LUKE 12:22–34

'do not worry about your life, what you will eat; or about your body, what you will wear.' (v22)

Over the years I have spent time with hundreds of people whose major struggle was that they were victims of fear. Many of them had fear take root when, as children, their parents would try to control them through unhealthy fear. To implant unhealthy fear in the mind of a child is a crime against the child. When adults attempt to rule children, or anyone else for that matter, by fear, then fear rules the child – and the adult. Sadly, it remains there even when the child becomes an adult.

While we understand that there is a healthy as well as an unhealthy fear, this is not true of worry. My dictionary defines worry as 'a period spent in over-anxious concern'. It is not wrong to be concerned about issues that trouble us, but when we allow our concern to paralyse us and drain us of the energy we need to face the other issues of the day, then we live dangerously. The issue with worry is that it does not change anything, except you. American philosopher William James said, 'If you believe that worrying long enough will change a past or future event then you are residing on another planet with a different reality system.'

FURTHER STUDY

Psa. 23:1–6;
Luke 10:38–42

1. How did David avoid being a victim of fear?

2. What was Jesus' counsel to Martha?

One medical doctor remarked, 'Worry is a form of atheism.' A person who worries is, in effect, saying, 'God is no longer there so I'll have to take matters into my own hands.' When we worry we are really thinking, 'God doesn't care. Why doesn't He do something?' The result? We take matters into our own hands or experience an inability to meet the difficulty when it comes. *Worry is a responsibility God never intended us to carry.* Worry is like a rocking chair – it makes you go backwards and forwards but it does not get you anywhere.

Lord God, I see how pointless it is to worry, and I therefore turn with eager heart and mind from the devastation to the deliverance. Help me believe that You are always near. In Jesus' name. Amen.

CWR Ministry Events

PLEASE PRAY FOR THE TEAM

DATE	EVENT	PLACE	PRESENTER(S)
6 Jan	BA Counselling Year 1 resumes	Pilgrim Hall	Waverley Abbey College team
13 Jan	BA Counselling Year 3 resumes	PH	Waverley Abbey College team
13 Jan	MA Counselling Year 1 resumes	Waverley Abbey House	Waverley Abbey College team
16 Jan	BA Counselling Year 4 resumes	PH	Waverley Abbey College team
20 Jan	BA Counselling Year 2 resumes	PH	Waverley Abbey College team
20 Jan	MA Relational Counselling and Psychotherapy resumes	WAH	Waverley Abbey College team
23–27 Jan	January Country Break	PH	Ewart Helyar and Pilgrim Hall team
26 Jan	Refreshing Your Spiritual Life	WAH	Andy Peck
26 Jan	MA Counselling Year 2 resumes	WAH	Waverley Abbey College team
4 Feb	Winter Glory Conference	Kettering Conference Centre	Lynette Brooks and Rosalyn Derges
9 Feb	Structuring Pastoral Care	WAH	Andy Peck
21 Feb	Prayer Breakfast	PH	Pilgrim Hall team
23 Feb	Sharing Jesus	WAH	Andy Peck

We would also appreciate prayer for our ongoing ministry in Singapore and Cambodia, as well as the many regional events that we are embarking on this year.

For further information and a full list of CWR's courses, seminars and events, call **+44 (0)1252 784719** or visit **www.cwr.org.uk/courses**

You can also download our free Prayer Track, which includes daily prayers, from **www.cwr.org.uk/free-resources**

Steps to deliverance

FOR READING & MEDITATION – JOHN 5:1–15

'When Jesus saw him lying there ... he asked him,
"Do you want to get well?"' (v6)

When I say to you that with God's help you can be free of fear and worry, I mean it. There are many hundreds of Christians around the world who can testify to the fact that fear and worry no longer control them. Here are some suggestions for you, gleaned from things others say have helped them to gain their freedom.

(1) Admit to yourself that you are fearful or worried. You don't have to pretend that you are not afraid or not worried. The Christian way is one of complete honesty. Do not attempt to wave a magic wand over your fears and tell yourself you are not afraid.

FURTHER STUDY

Gen. 32:7–12;
Luke 12:11–12;
John 16:33

1. How did Jacob's prayer combat his fear?

2. What encouragement did Jesus give His followers?

(2) Ask yourself (although it is a difficult question) the question Jesus asked the man in today's passage: 'Do you want to get well?' The longing to be free has to be there. You could also ask: Do I really want to give up the thing I am afraid of? Sometimes people hold on to a fear because of the pay-off they get from it through sympathy and attention.

(3) It is important to surrender the thing you fear to God. Turn it right over to Him and ask for His help in solving the situation. In your own hands the thing you fear is a problem; in His hands it is a possibility.

(4) Remind yourself that every fear, every trouble has been defeated by the One you follow – Jesus Christ. Say to every fear and worry, 'I am not afraid of you and I am not going to be controlled by you.' Remember, Jesus walks alongside you, and He is the One who mastered everything so that you need not be mastered by anything. Never forget that you will be defeated by fear and worry only if you consent to it. Don't consent – connect. Connect with Jesus and all will be well.

Father God, help me to acknowledge the weakness of my own will and gratefully accept the strength You offer. I long to be free of all fears and worries. In You I am more than a match for anything. I am so thankful. Amen.

One day at a time

FOR READING & MEDITATION – MATTHEW 6:25–34

'Therefore do not worry about tomorrow, for tomorrow will worry about itself.' (v34)

Today we continue looking at the steps that can help us gain freedom from worry and fear.

(5) Understand that the thing that is causing you fear or worry is not as bad as the fear itself. If you keep the centre of your life intact then you can come back from any setback. If the centre of your life is *not* intact then you will continue to be 'tossed about' by happenings, both real and imaginary. The person who fights life's battles free from fear fights only one enemy – the one in front of them. But the person who fights with fear fights three things: the real problem, the imaginary problem created by the fear and the fear itself. And the worst of these is the fear.

(6) Direct your attention to Jesus. Whatever holds your focus holds you. If Jesus gains your attention He will gain you. When fear and worry vie for your attention, deliberately turn your attention to Jesus. Fill your mind with faith – faith in Him – because perfect love drives out fear.

(7) Learn to meet today, today. Jesus gave us a tremendous clue as to how to live a life free from fear and worry when He spoke the words in today's key verse. He was not saying there are no troubles to be met, for life can be full of them. 'Into every life a little rain must fall,' said one poet. How true. But don't bring forward the troubles of tomorrow into today. Do you think this advice is impossible to follow? Jesus would never have given this instruction if it were not possible. Ask for His help in this matter. It's surprising how things thought impossible become possible when God is brought into the situation.

FURTHER STUDY

Mark 9:2–8; Heb. 13:8

1. How were the disciples encouraged to focus on Jesus?

2. Make the promise in Hebrews your confession of faith today.

Lord, help me see that each day You give me a load that I can manage. Help me not to increase my burden by adding to it tomorrow's problems, reducing my ability to deal with the legitimate tasks of today. Please forgive me. Amen.

Passive – active

FOR READING & MEDITATION – ISAIAH 30:12–18

'in quietness and trust is your strength' (v15)

For one more day, we consider some steps that can help us be free from worry and fear.

(8) Repeat these words taken from Scripture as often as you can: 'In quietness and trust is my strength.' Notice that *two* things are mentioned here: quietness and trust. You can learn to quieten everything in your heart. That can happen when you wait before God in prayer. Still your soul before Him and drink in His quiet strength. Allow the healing quiet of Jesus to fill you, bathing your restless mind in His perfect peace. But quietness is not enough – there is also trust. Quietness is inactive, but trust is active. Reach out to your heavenly Father and put your hand in His. Make this your prayer: 'Lord, nothing can happen any day of my life that You and I can't handle together.' Then step out in trust.

(9) Choose to give yourself to others. When you have handed over your fears and worries to God, so that your heart does not become a vacuum, fill it with love for others. The purpose of living, as I have often said before, is to have loving involvement with God and loving involvement with others. Jesus says in Matthew 22:39 that we are to love our neighbours as ourselves, and that means what we love for ourselves we ought to wish for others also. Do you love to be free of fear? Then long for others to be free from it as well. The two heartbeats of life are giving and receiving. You receive from God and you give to others. Passive, active. You take in and you give out. So whatever the ways in which God blesses you, seek to share the blessing with others. These suggestions will help you on your journey towards freedom.

FURTHER STUDY

Psa. 46:1–11;
Mark 12:28–34

1. How does God encourage us to *really* know He is God?

2. For what did Jesus commend the teacher of the law?

Father, I see that none of the precious gifts You give me are to be kept for my own use – but passed on to others. Freely I have received; help me freely to give. In Jesus' name. Amen.

CWR

Helping you live life God's way

...through coming alongside others

God's Church has the wonderful potential to be a community where we can come alongside one another, journey through life together and share the insights we glean when overcoming life's trials.

CWR's six-week series **Paraclesis: Journeying Together** by Trevor J. Partridge, enables churches to develop this culture of care within their congregations. Trevor explains the concept further in his accompanying book *Love with Skin On...*

Help we receive from God isn't simply for our own benefit. Our hard times not only give us opportunities to receive His grace and comfort, but they open a door of opportunity to share our experiences with others.

By connecting through our experiences, we can reach out to others in our church and community, and come alongside them – significantly impacting a lost and broken world.

Visit **www.paraclesis.org.uk** to discover more.

paraclesis
Coming alongside others

To all who struggle

FOR READING & MEDITATION – HEBREWS 10:1–18

'Their sins and lawless acts I will remember no more.' (v17)

Now we think about another area of life in which we need divine help: freedom from past indiscretions and sins. I am amazed at the number of Christians who, even though they have asked God for forgiveness for an indiscretion they have committed, still feel emotional turmoil each time they remember it.

All of us have needed to repent. Why is it that some individuals who have committed serious wrongdoing can find forgiveness from God and then walk on without ever looking back, but others, who have committed equally grave acts and experienced the same forgiveness, find themselves unable to forget? Some psychologists say it has to do with the sensitivity and make-up of the personality. One Christian psychologist claims that it is often due to a low sense of worth. The person concerned feels they are too bad to be forgiven. Some spiritual counsellors believe the problem has to do with pride: 'Me? Having done such a thing as that? How could it ever have happened?'

FURTHER STUDY

Psa. 32:1–2;
Micah 7:18–20;
Acts 13:38–41

1. Of what kind of God does the prophet speak?

2. Through whom does our forgiveness come?

To all who struggle in this way I want to say that I believe God can help us put the past in its right perspective so that, even though we may never forget a devastating incident or circumstance, we will not be emotionally overwhelmed by it. It is possible to remember without reliving it because we have experienced the joy of realised forgiveness. This new year you can know how to enlist God's aid so that you can move forward with the light step of a forgiven man or woman. Our text tells us God does not remember a sin that has been forgiven in the sense that He does not hold it against us. You also need not; this is the truth of a loving, forgiving God.

God my Father, I know I have been forgiven; help me feel forgiven, I pray. Let my heart as well as my head experience forgiveness, and give me strength over any past sins that may still trouble me. In Jesus' name. Amen.

Holding the clothes

FOR READING & MEDITATION – ACTS 7:54–60

'Meanwhile, the witnesses laid their clothes at the feet of a young man named Saul.' (v58)

The apostle Paul was definitely a man with a past. The first time Paul is mentioned in the New Testament is in connection with a judicial murder. Without doubt, Paul is one of the greatest figures in the Early Church after Jesus, but when we first catch sight of him he is implicated in a crime. Stephen had defended himself with great skill before the members of the Sanhedrin, but even so they rushed him out of the city and stoned him to death. It was a form of execution almost as terrible as crucifixion. The victim was flung against a wall and huge stones were then hurled at him until he was literally pounded to death. And Paul was there, holding the clothes. No one could accuse him of throwing a stone. But he was an accessory before and after the fact. Though he might have walked away saying, 'I did not do it,' yet the blood of Stephen was on his hands.

Paul was a sensitive man. Do you not think that, following his conversion, he regretted his involvement in Stephen's death? Yet after he had found forgiveness he was able to put his past behind him as he wrote, 'But one thing I do: Forgetting what is behind and straining towards what is ahead, I press on towards the goal to win the prize for which God has called me heavenwards in Christ Jesus' (Phil. 3:13–14).

He has set an example and shows us the way forward. Get right with God, forget the things that are behind and press forward towards the goal. The secret is to know without a shadow of doubt that you have been forgiven by God. You have to take His word on this matter. He means what He says when He tells you, 'I forgive you.' Never doubt this.

FURTHER STUDY

Isa. 44:21–23;
Acts 22:14–21;
Col. 2:13–15

1. What does God call Israel to remember?

2. How was Paul's sinful past dealt with by God?

My Father and my God, may no cloud of doubt settle on my soul in relation to this matter of divine forgiveness. If there is an issue here to be settled then help me to settle it today. In Jesus' name. Amen.

'I'm forgiven'

FOR READING & MEDITATION – PSALM 103:1–22

'who forgives all your sins and heals all your diseases' (v3)

Following yesterday's meditation, when we noted that Paul was able to forget what was in the past, perhaps you are thinking to yourself, 'How do I forget?' Isn't it unreasonable to expect to be able to forget a significant situation from the past? Sometimes the changed circumstances a past sin might have caused cry out aloud with every day that comes.

When I was a young pastor, I sat with an old man who was terminally ill. Each time his wife came into the room he would follow her with his eyes, and when she left the room he would burst into tears. I asked him what was wrong. 'Whenever I look at her I can't help but remember the many times I hit her and blackened her eyes,' he confessed. 'It stopped long ago, after my conversion, but I can't help thinking what a bad man I was to hurt her. I know she has forgiven me but I can't forgive myself.' I heard, as we talked together, his remark about forgiving himself and gently suggested that perhaps his issue was more that he hadn't fully realised he had been forgiven.

This issue of *realised* forgiveness is something I have often written about, and many people respond to say that the *realisation* of forgiveness has yet to reach their heart. It is one thing to be forgiven; it is another thing to *realise* it. Our churches are filled with people whose realisation of forgiveness is incomplete. If it were complete, we would act quite differently. The old man to whom I have just referred took my words as eagerly as a drowning man reaches out for a lifebelt. He died a few days later in perfect peace, I am glad to say, his last words being 'I'm forgiven! I'm forgiven!'

FURTHER STUDY

Psa. 130:1–8;
Eph. 1:3–8

1. How should we react to God's forgiveness, according to the psalmist?

2. Meditate on Paul's description of a God who forgives.

Lord, how thankful I am for this message of divine forgiveness. I sing with the hymnist, 'My past, not in part, but the whole, is nailed to the cross and I bear it no more. It is well, it is well with my soul.' Amen.

No sin need rule

FOR READING & MEDITATION – PSALM 119:129–136

*'Direct my footsteps according to your word;
let no sin rule over me.' (v133)*

Yesterday I made reference to an elderly man who was paralysed by his past wrongdoing. Let me tell you, today, about another person with this problem, whom I met when I was speaking at a church retreat.

A middle-aged woman, who was in fact the worship leader for the retreat, asked to see me for some counselling. She began by saying, 'I hope this doesn't shock you too much but I am addicted to alcohol and unable to break with it. I even had to slip out to a local pub for a drink before I could share this with you.' 'How did it begin … this addiction to alcohol?' I enquired. 'It began when I had an abortion,' she replied, 'not for medical reasons. After the abortion, I felt as if my child was saying, "You have robbed me of life." I turned to drink so that I could forget. I have never been able to put this behind me. Will it haunt me for ever?' Thankfully, after counselling, this lady came to a full realisation of God's forgiveness and later told me in a letter that she was able to recollect the event without being overwhelmed by a sense of shame. Regret over what had happened, yes; an ongoing feeling of shame, no.

FURTHER STUDY

Hosea 14:1–9;
Rom. 12:9;
1 Pet. 2:11–12

1. To those who return, what is God's promise?

2. What should be our attitude towards sin of any kind?

I am going to spend a little time over the next few days sharing with you some of the principles others have found useful when seeking to help people struggling to resolve this issue of past behaviour and actions. The first principle is this: don't minimise the sin. Never say of a sin, 'It isn't important.' That is not true, for the Bible tells us plainly, 'The wages of sin is death' (Rom. 6:23). A deadly thing, such as sin, is not made innocuous simply by giving it an inoffensive name.

Lord God, help me never to minimise sin. Give me the courage to call sin by its rightful name and see it not just as something that breaks Your laws but that breaks Your heart also. In Jesus' name. Amen.

Self-deceived

FOR READING & MEDITATION – PSALM 51:1–19

'Have mercy on me, O God ... according to your great compassion blot out my transgressions.' (v1)

We began yesterday to look at some of the principles that can help us gain freedom from past failures and sins. First, we must never minimise sin. Often we create new labels for sin. Some refer to adultery as an affair, or to what is essentially a promiscuous lifestyle as 'sleeping around'. A great many people, I have found, never enter into the freedom of forgiveness because they gloss over their behaviour, so simply feel they need to be excused rather than forgiven. The first trap to avoid, then, in dealing with issues from the past is not to minimise sin.

And don't look for excuses to justify your actions – be prepared to take full responsibility. Admission of the seriousness of an issue is the prerequisite to finding full and free forgiveness.

FURTHER STUDY

Jonah 3:1–10;
Luke 15:20–24

1. How did God respond to Nineveh's repentance?

2. How did the father respond to his younger son?

Once you see sin for what it really is, then the next step is to go to God in repentance. When King David committed adultery with Bathsheba and arranged the death of her husband, he was so self-deceived that he did not see his actions as self-centred and destructive (see 2 Sam. 11:1–12:13). Had the prophet Nathan argued with David over his sin, the king might have retorted, 'Bathsheba should have been more careful about where she bathed. She is to blame for exposing herself within sight of my palace.' After Nathan's pointed parable did its work, however, David came to see the sinfulness of his behaviour and only then did the cry of Psalm 51 arise.

If the heart is to know full and free forgiveness, repentance must be deep and sincere. Repentance is far more than being sorry for your sin; it is being sorry also for the condition of your heart that brought about the sin.

God help me understand even more fully that I will not see the need for repentance unless I grasp the enormity of sin. You long for me to be free of the things that soil my soul; deepen my awareness of this, I pray. In Jesus' name. Amen.

Stop brooding

FOR READING & MEDITATION – 1 JOHN 1:1–10

'the blood of Jesus, his Son, purifies us from all sin.' (v7)

Today we continue focusing on the principles we can follow if we are to gain freedom over some sin or failure in the past that still gnaws away in our personality. Let's remind ourselves of what we have covered so far. Firstly, do not minimise the sin. Second, go to God in repentance. Next, do not brood over the past.

Brooding over the past is not only harmful and destructive but can also exacerbate regret and a tendency towards hurt pride. As we discovered earlier, what we are really saying when brooding over a past indiscretion is this: 'How could I have ever done that?' Note the stress on the 'I'.

Some self-loathing will be there too. Self-loathing is one possible way of diverting the pain of unresolved guilt. We recognise it as our old nature because it tries to deal with matters psychologically instead of spiritually. Self-loathing and self-contempt may act as temporary painkillers for the soul but they do not resolve the problem. God delights to forgive; never forget that.

Think for a moment what divine forgiveness means. Because of what Jesus did on Calvary, every sin you have ever committed can be wiped clean from God's records. What is more, Jesus' sacrifice on the cross enables you to be free not only from the consequences of sin but also its control. God does not require payment for sin twice – once by His Son and once by us. Brooding and punishing yourself may be the sign of a subconscious desire to pay back a debt to God by your own suffering. The debt has been paid for you at Calvary, so receive the forgiveness offered and rejoice in it.

FURTHER STUDY

1 Tim. 1:12–17; Rev. 1:4–6

1. How did Paul view his past?

2. Starting with the apostle John's words, offer praise to God.

Father, how can I thank You enough for this good news? No words can adequately express my gratitude. My heart is full of humble adoration, gratitude and praise. In Jesus' name. Amen.

Made to forget

FOR READING & MEDITATION – GENESIS 41:41–57

*'God has made me forget all my trouble and all
my father's household.' (v51)*

A final suggestion I would like to make on this issue of walking free from the past is that God not only forgives sin but He is also the master at taking what was meant for bad and turning it to good. Consider this: the crucifixion was the worst thing that has happened in the universe but God has turned it into the best thing that has happened in the universe. The God who is mighty in creation is mighty also in transformation. I promise you that if you take your sin to Him – really take it to Him and do not hug it to yourself – He can turn your setbacks into springboards.

**FURTHER
STUDY**

1 Cor. 6:9–11;
Titus 3:3–8

1. How has the past life of the Corinthians been transformed?

2. List all that God has done to save us from past sin.

And how does He do that? By using the cleansed memory of it to drive the engine of your will, to quicken your compassion towards others and to show God's tender heart to the fallen who might have gained from other Christians the false impression that God is hard and unforgiving. Can you see what I mean now when I say God can do more with sin than just forgive it?

Before moving on, let's remind ourselves what we have been saying concerning this matter of past sins. If you are tormented by some memory of the past, then ask yourself: Have I been to God with it? Has my repentance been sincere? Have I renounced all sin and am I living in the light of God? Have I accepted God's full and free forgiveness? And have I learned the lesson that my behaviour has taught me? If you can say 'Yes' to all those questions, then forget the past. In God's name put it behind you once and for all. And if you have trouble forgetting it then ask God to do for you what Joseph declared God did for him: 'God has *made* me forget.'

Today I draw a veil over the past. What You have forgiven I want to forget. Please *make* me forget. From now on I will look to the future, not to the past. Lead on heavenly Father. I will follow. Amen.

'The pleasures of resentment'

'rid yourselves of all malice and all deceit, hypocrisy, envy, and slander of every kind.' (2:1)

Another matter we need to think about is how to gain freedom from the problem of lingering resentment. I keep returning to this issue because I am amazed at the number of Christians who are bound by this emotion. It dominates the lives of many people – even those who have been Christians for many years.

When I was deeply involved in counselling I found that lingering resentment played a major part in the struggles of eight out of ten people I met in the counselling room. C.S. Lewis observed that there is pleasure in resentment. Writing in his book *The Four Loves* he said, 'If anyone says he does not know the pleasures of resentment he is either a liar or a saint.' I have come to the conclusion that resentment is not a primary emotion. What happens, I think, is that we get hurt, and because hurt is such an unpleasant feeling we cover it over with resentment. Resentment is a more agreeable feeling than hurt as it puts us into the driving seat. It gives us a feeling of power, of being in control. It is like scratching ourselves when we get an itch; the relief is pleasant but only as an alternative to the irritation. Perhaps this is what C.S. Lewis meant when he spoke of 'the pleasures of resentment'. Lewis talked also about 'how madly one cherishes this base part as if it were one's dearest possession'. And make no mistake about it – it is a base part of us.

While waiting in line in a supermarket once, I heard a woman comment, 'She burns me up.' I thought to myself, 'Whoever this woman is, if you let her continue burning you up then you will be the loser.' With the help of Jesus we can learn to be free from resentment before it masters us.

FURTHER STUDY

Gen. 4:1–8; James 1:13–15, 19–21

1. Why did Cain's resentment fester?

2. What is James' counsel and teaching on anger?

Heavenly Father, I know You have fashioned me for love, not resentment. Save me from allowing the self-brewed poison of resentment to fester in my heart. In Jesus' name. Amen.

The only option

'A heart at peace gives life to the body, but envy rots the bones.' (v30)

We are continuing to look at an insidious poison that, if not released, will reduce us to sour, sullen, damaged souls – lingering resentment. A medical doctor once commented, 'Resentment puts the whole physical and mental system on a war basis instead of a peace basis.' Resentment can, I believe, make a person physically ill and will certainly wear them out. Sadly, I once witnessed the effect that being consumed with resentment had on a man – resentment of a relative who had sued him. Within a year or two, he was dead.

FURTHER STUDY

Psa. 32:3–5;
3 John
1–4,11–14

1. What are the effects of unconfessed sin on the body?

2. What is John's prayer for, and his instructions to, Gaius?

When I was working as a pastor, I found that often after I had helped sick people deal with resentment the illness would disappear. I can't tell you the number of times people said to me, 'Pastor, I believe if I had dealt with that issue before I would not have got ill.' Though I have had no medical training, I have questioned many of my medical friends about the effect of the mind on the body. All of them have had stories to tell of people who were suffering because of lingering resentment. Resentment not only leaves splinters in the soul, it leaves splinters in the body as well.

The text before us today tells us that 'A heart at peace gives life to the body, but envy rots the bones.' The same could be said of resentment. If we don't deal with our resentment it can cause physical difficulties. Good will is good for you; bad will is bad for you. There was an interesting article by a neurologist who explored the ingenious ways humans express distress, which ranged from headaches to paralysis. Please resolve before God to be rid of any lingering resentment before it gets rid of you.

Father, I see that Your way is inescapable. If I attempt to escape from it then I find I am escaping from life. Help me to come to terms with this fact and take Your way – always. In Jesus' name. Amen.

What's eating you?

FOR READING & MEDITATION – JOB 5:1–13

'Resentment kills a fool, and envy slays the simple.' (v2)

A missionary who returned home because of a mysterious illness that his doctor could not diagnose told me that the cause of the illness was hidden resentment. 'What my doctor did not know,' he said, 'was that I was harbouring a deep resentment against a colleague on the mission field. I came to a point where I knew I could not go on like this – the resentment was killing me. So I surrendered it to God and within days I was well again.' His doctor, on seeing the difference in him, said laughingly, 'I don't know what has happened to you, but it seems you are well enough now to go and dig trenches.'

Sometimes, however, the resentment we carry is not against people but against situations that we find disagreeable. One woman found herself in a job she did not like. Every time she went to work she fumed inwardly until she developed serious stomach trouble. Though she was given all kinds of treatment, nothing helped. Then one morning, while reading *Every Day with Jesus*, she came across this statement: 'It may be not what you are eating but what is eating you that is your problem.' She got down on her knees, surrendered her resentment to God, and immediately felt better. The woman, a New Zealander, took the opportunity to tell me this when I autographed a book for her some years ago in a bookshop in Auckland.

Am I speaking to someone today, somewhere in the world, who is chewing on resentment that, in turn, is contributing to your ill health? Decide to have done with it – now. No one can afford to carry resentment. It takes too much of a toll. As a doctor once said, 'You chew on your own tongue when you chew on resentment.'

FURTHER STUDY

Psa. 38:1–10, 21–22;
1 Thess. 5:15–24

1. What is David's complaint and what is his prayer?

2. Reflect on Paul's admonition and meditate on his prayer.

Father, help me to never harbour resentment when it is clearly harmful to my soul and body. I am being taught that I am made for love, not resentment. Help me, my Father, to be a truly forgiving person. Amen.

CWR

Helping others live life God's way

If you would like to support the work of CWR, here's a little more about what we do and how you can help.

CWR's ministry extends around the globe. Our resources are shipped regularly to Australia and New Zealand, where thousands of free Bible reading notes are going into prisons each month. Our partner in Nigeria prints and distributes around 100,000 daily devotionals six times a year. We train counsellors in Singapore, provide resources in Malaysia, and offer our teaching in Cambodia.

In the UK, we provide engaging resources for men, women, children and young people, especially created for them to help them discover God's Word and apply it to their lives.

With your generosity, and God's abundant blessing, CWR can continue to provide opportunities such as these for countless people every day.

To donate, please use the order form at the back of these notes or visit **www.cwr.org.uk/donate**

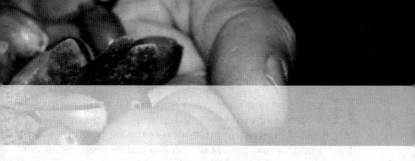

Give, and it will be given to you. A good measure, pressed down, shaken together and running over, will be poured into your lap. For with the measure you use, it will be measured to you. (Luke 6:38)

Partner with us

Would you like to partner with CWR and help us to encourage individuals, equip churches, train counsellors, inspire prisoners and cross borders with God's Word? You can become a Partner from as little as 50p a day (£15 per month). As a Partner, you will be invited to special events to hear more about the charity and will receive regular updates on the work we are achieving together.

To become a CWR Partner please call **01252 784709** or email **partners@cwr.org.uk**

On behalf of all those who will draw closer to God because of your generosity, support and prayers, CWR would like to say thank you.

Don't miss it

FOR READING & MEDITATION – MARK 3:1–6

'He looked round at them in anger and, deeply distressed at their stubborn hearts, said to the man, "Stretch out your hand."' (v5)

Having seen how damaging resentment is to the personality we now ask ourselves: What must we do to be rid of resentment? First, accept that all resentment is wrong even if it is seemingly justified. Many seek to justify their resentment by calling it 'righteous indignation'. As I may have mentioned before, when I was young I thought that if anyone held resentment against me it was *unrighteous* indignation, but if I held resentment against them it was *righteous* indignation! Since then I have learned differently!

FURTHER STUDY

Eph. 3:14–19; James 3:13–18

1. Meditate on the main focus of Paul's prayer.

2. Contrast heavenly wisdom with earthly wisdom.

Of course, there *is* such a thing as righteous indignation. Jesus demonstrated it in the synagogue, as we see from our reading today. The account says that He was deeply distressed at the people's stubbornness. This is one way to tell if our indignation is righteous or unrighteous: when we are distressed at what is happening to others, and not responding simply to what is happening to us, then the indignation can be described as righteous.

Next, realise, as Hebrews 12:15 tells us, that resentment arises as a consequence of our missing the grace of God. 'See to it that no one misses the grace of God,' this verse warns us, 'and that no bitter root grows up to cause trouble and defile many.' Grace flows towards us every moment of our lives, enabling us to respond to all that happens in a godly way. If we ignore that grace and therefore miss it, then a root of bitterness is likely to spring up. It's no good saying, 'I can't help being resentful. It's my nature.' God's grace is available to help you overcome your natural instincts. It's there for you every time you are hurt. Don't miss it.

Lord, I know I simply must learn these lessons if I am to thrive in Your kingdom. May nothing take root in me that does not come from You. In Jesus' name. Amen.

Don't wrestle – nestle

FOR READING & MEDITATION – EPHESIANS 4:17–32

'*"In your anger do not sin": Do not let the sun go down
while you are still angry*' (v26)

A further thing that helps us to gain freedom from resentment is determining that, even if we can't stop resentment arising in our hearts, we will make sure it does not linger there. I am aware that today's text refers to anger and not resentment (anger is a flare-up of the emotions, resentment is a slow burn), but the principle is the same. Deal with it before it begins to deal with you. Simply confess your resentment to God, surrender it to Him, tell Him you don't want it to rule your life and put the whole matter into His hands.

Whatever you do, don't attempt to deal with resentment in your own strength. If you try to suppress it, all you will do is push it into the subconscious where it will continue to burn and smoulder. Remember that you never bury any emotion dead – you bury it alive. And emotions, as I have said, can have a harmful effect on the body. In Christian terms, the need, as Corrie ten Boom used to say, is not to wrestle but to nestle.

Another principle to follow if we are to be free from lingering resentment is: forgive everyone against whom you feel resentment. This can be extremely challenging. Immediately after teaching the disciples the Lord's Prayer Jesus said, 'But if you do not forgive men their sins, your Father will not forgive your sins' (Matt. 6:15). The following statement, which I read in a commentary, pulled me up sharply: 'God cannot forgive the unforgiving. His hands are tied. His hands are released in forgiving us when we decide to forgive others who may have hurt us.' How powerful; if we refuse to forgive we break the bridge over which we ourselves must pass. Give yourself into your loving Father's hands today.

FURTHER STUDY

Mark 7:14–23;
Gal. 5:13–15

1. What does Jesus want us to understand?

2. What should we use our freedom for?

Gracious and forgiving God, help me to forgive others as freely and as fully as You forgive me. May I take forgiveness with one hand and give it with the other. In Jesus' name. Amen.

'I will grant the pardon'

FOR READING & MEDITATION – PHILIPPIANS 2:1–11

'Your attitude should be the same as that of Christ Jesus' (v5)

For one more day we will linger on this issue of forgiveness. Since we ourselves have been forgiven, we can now learn to extend forgiveness towards those around us. When we refuse to forgive others, we inhibit God's forgiveness reaching us. It is not that God does not want to forgive us; the problem is that we are putting ourselves in a position where we are unable to fully receive His forgiveness. We read in today's text that we are to treat each other in the same way that Jesus treats us. And how does He treat us? With kindness, consideration and forgiveness. When He forgives, He forgives wholly; when He forgets, He forgets wholly.

FURTHER STUDY

Gen. 50:15–21;
Rom. 12:14–21

1. How did Joseph reassure his brothers?

2. How does Paul suggest that we can 'overcome evil with good'?

You may well find this final suggestion of mine difficult, but, with God's help, try to do good to anyone against whom you have held resentment. The story is told in the USA of a preacher who walked fifty miles to plead with George Washington to spare the life of a man who had been sentenced to death for dereliction of duty. 'I am sorry,' said Washington after listening to the preacher's plea, 'but I cannot grant the request for your friend's pardon.' 'But he's not my friend,' the preacher responded. 'For some reason he has made himself my greatest enemy.' 'Surely you are not pleading for your enemy,' Washington exclaimed. 'I am,' replied the preacher. 'Then,' said Washington, 'I will grant the pardon.' I believe if you learn and then live out the principles I have outlined, not only will they prevent you from becoming a sour, morose and embittered soul but they will transform you into the image of Jesus. The more you love, the more like Him you will become.

Lord Jesus, You not only suffered for those who hammered You to the cross, You prayed for them also. Help me, when wronged, to forgive my enemies too – and to pray for them. For Your own dear name's sake. Amen.

He is still watching

FOR READING & MEDITATION – MARK 12:41–44

'Jesus sat down opposite the place where the offerings were put and watched the crowd' (v41)

We turn our attention now to another area of life that can, if we are not intentional in our approach to it, master us. I am referring, of course, to money. No one can live a fully effective life unless they have control over their money. The account before us today says, 'Jesus sat down opposite the place where the offerings were put and *watched*'. He is watching still! These next few days will be tremendously challenging as, with Jesus watching us, we shall review our attitude to money.

In the parable Jesus told about the sower and the seed He said, 'The one who received the seed that fell among the thorns is the man who hears the word, but the worries of this life and the deceitfulness of wealth choke it, making it unfruitful' (Matt. 13:22). Notice that two things choke the seed: the worries of life and the deceitfulness of wealth. The Living Bible translates the phrase 'deceitfulness of wealth' as the 'longing for money'. Jesus did not say riches are an enemy of the soul, but allowing the longing for it to take over us leads to trouble. Anyone who delights in riches because of the good that can be achieved through them will be blessed, but those who delight in riches for their own sake – when they become an end in themselves – will hear Jesus say, as He said to the people of His day, 'You cannot serve both God and Money' (Matt. 6:24).

Though you cannot serve God and money you can, of course, serve God with money. Ask yourself this question: Is money my master or my servant? Before you answer, think again about today's text: 'Jesus sat opposite the place where the offerings were put and watched'...

FURTHER STUDY

1 Tim. 6:6–10;
1 Pet. 5:1–4

1. What warning does Paul give to those who love money?

2. What qualities does Peter outline for elders?

Father, You who sent Your Son into the world so that I might be free, help me be free from the bondage to money, I pray. I would have everything I possess dedicated to Your purposes. In Jesus' name. Amen.

A sharp issue

FOR READING & MEDITATION – LUKE 12:13–21

'Watch out! Be on your guard against all kinds of greed; a man's life does not consist in the abundance of his possessions.' (v15)

'When we face the question of material possessions,' said one writer, 'we face this sharp issue: either we will transform the material into the image of the spiritual or the material will transform us into its own image.' Some Christians allow the material to govern their lives and dominate their thinking. They begin to resemble the god they serve and become as metallic as the coins they handle.

The poet Edna St Vincent Millay, in Sonnet XLIII, spoke about a heart in which there is no summer:

FURTHER STUDY

Psa. 135:15–18;
Matt. 6:19–21;
1 John 2:15–17

1. What happens to those who trust idols?

2. How does John exhort his readers?

I cannot say what loves have come and gone,
I only know that summer sang in me
A little while, that in me sings no more.

There is no summer in a heart set on material wealth.

I came across the following fable: A leopard was shot and its skin made into a coat. It was put on display in a shop window and its price marked up at $5,000. One day the rest of the family of leopards was out walking. Stopping at the shop window, they recognised the skin of their father. One of the young leopards remarked, 'He was better off when he wasn't worth so much. At least then he was alive!'

I have known many Christians who have found wealth, but because they have developed a greater love for their possessions than for their Master, their souls have become dead. 'I've learned how to make money,' said one millionaire who later committed suicide, 'but I have not learned how to live.' His life could not be sustained by material goods. Neither can ours – so today choose to put your God above your possessions. God is always available for financial advice!

Father, help me understand that I am made in Your image and that I cannot live – live effectively – if I try to live in the image of the material. Save me from trying. In Jesus' name. Amen.

Sacrificial giving

MON
23 JAN

FOR READING & MEDITATION – ACTS 4:32–37

*'There were no needy persons among them. For ... those who owned
lands or houses sold them' (v34)*

The great missionary David Livingstone once said, 'I will
place no value on anything that I have or possess except
in relation to the kingdom of Christ. If anything I have will
advance that kingdom, it shall be given or kept, as by giving
or keeping it I shall best promote the glory of Him to whom I
owe all my hopes both for time and eternity.' One commentator
called this attitude of Livingstone's 'streamlining your life for
kingdom purposes'.

A famous American multi-millionaire and philanthropist
visited China to see if the money he had given to
Christian causes there was being used wisely. On
his travels he came across a town where there was a
newly built chapel. He asked if some of his money had
been used for that purpose and was told that it had not
been needed there. Later he discovered that a farmer
had sold one of his oxen to complete the building of
the chapel, so he visited the farmer. When he arrived,
he saw a strange sight: an ox and a young man yoked
together. Expressing his surprise, the farmer explained,
'When the chapel needed to be finished my son had no
money to give so he said, "Let us sell one of the oxen
and I will take the yoke of the ox." We did and gave
the money to the chapel.'

The millionaire philanthropist said, 'I realised then that,
although I knew the meaning of giving, I did not know the
meaning of *sacrificial* giving. I offered up a prayer in the middle
of that field – a prayer that the Lord would let me be hitched to
a "plough" so that I too might know the joy of sacrificial giving.'
All giving is good but *sacrificial* giving brings a special joy that
only those who practise it experience.

**FURTHER
STUDY**

2 Sam.
24:18–25;
2 Cor. 8:1–5

1. What was
David's reaction
to Araunah's
offer?

2. For what does
Paul commend
the Macedonian
churches?

**Father, I live in an acquisitive society where worth is often judged
by wealth. Give me a new perspective. Increase my awareness of
my attachment to my money, I pray, and, above all, help me be a
sacrificial giver. In Jesus' name. Amen.**

Our Master's money

FOR READING & MEDITATION – MATTHEW 25:14–30

*'But the man who had received the one talent went off, dug a hole in
the ground and hid his master's money.' (v18)*

How can we be free from being controlled by money and ensure that it does not get mastery over us? Here are some suggestions. First, transfer everything you possess to God. If you have not already done this, do it now. Say, 'Lord, You are the possessor, I am the steward.' When God is recognised as the Owner then we have the right perspective; if we regard ourselves as owners then we have the wrong perspective.

Next, give at least a tenth of all you earn to God. Many Bible teachers say tithing dates back to the giving of the law, but actually tithing was in existence before this time (see Gen. 14:20). Tithing is a very good principle with which to begin. However, let's not think that when we have given a tithe we have fulfilled our responsibility to give. The remaining nine-tenths belong to God also, and it is our duty, privilege and pleasure to manage that well for Him. What we give over and above the tithe is an offering. Some may not be able to give more than a tithe. God knows everyone's financial situation. Our task is to come before Him as good stewards and ask for wisdom to know how to handle what really is our Master's money.

**FURTHER
STUDY**

Gen. 28:20–22;
Acts 20:32–35;
2 Cor. 8:10–15

1. What did
Jacob vow?

2. What words
of Jesus does
Paul quote?

I have settled this issue of money by asking myself a simple question: How much of His money does the Lord want me to keep for myself? Everything I needlessly spend on myself prevents some other person's need being met. I deprive that person and also deprive myself. When I help meet the needs of others through what is surplus to my needs then I help others physically and myself morally. That has been the guiding principle of my life for many years in relation to money. I commend it to you.

**Father, since I belong to You, and all I have belongs to You, then
everything is at Your disposal. Show me how much I should keep
for my own needs and what I should give to others. In Jesus' name.
Amen.**

The gift of giving

FOR READING & MEDITATION – ROMANS 12:1–8

'if it is contributing to the needs of others, let him give generously'
(v8)

Some people, as our text suggests, are specially gifted to make money and use it for the kingdom of God. What a difference these people make! If you are such a person – a businessman or woman or a highly paid professional – then may God guide you and give you the wisdom you need to be a good steward of our Saviour's money.

So far we have said two things help us to be free from the grip of money: transferring ownership of everything we have to God, and being clear where our own needs end and the needs of others begin. When you let go of your possessions and transfer ownership of them to God, then you become very conscious that you are only a steward. Money becomes a commodity to be used wisely and not a master.

As an aside, let me urge you to be careful about lending people money. Many a relationship has been broken because the person lent the money has been unable to repay the loan and, out of embarrassment, has ended the friendship. Sometimes it is better to just give money than to lend it. Always pray about such matters and ask Jesus to share with you His wisdom on the subject. However, while we are on this point, let me add that in certain situations the worst thing you can do is to give money because it can make the recipient dependent. If this is a possibility, it might be more help in the long run to give the person concerned an idea as to how they can help themselves. When you give, give because God has directed you to give, not because of an emotional response to an appeal. Giving is an investment in God's kingdom and a return is guaranteed, not necessarily in terms of wealth, but in increasing joy and happiness.

FURTHER STUDY

Acts 2:42–47;
1 Pet. 4:8–11

1. What characterised the Early Church?

2. In what ways does Peter suggest we can serve each other?

Father, I pray that You will root out anything that may be causing me to love money more than I love You. On my own I cannot cut those roots entirely but with Your help I can. In Jesus' name I ask this. Amen.

The joy of giving

FOR READING & MEDITATION – 2 CORINTHIANS 9:6–15

'Each man should give what he has decided ... to give, not reluctantly or under compulsion, for God loves a cheerful giver.' (v7)

The last thing I would like to say about not being controlled by money is this: be a joyful, not a reluctant giver. I heard one preacher say, 'Some people give like Moses' rock – only when they are struck. Some give like a sponge – only when they are squeezed. Others give like the flowers – because they love to give.' The happiest Christians I know are those whose lives are tipped in the direction of giving.

In the early days of my Christian life, I used to think that when preachers drew attention to the words 'It is more blessed to give than to receive' (Acts 20:35) they were using Scripture to manipulate people and boost their offerings. Now I have come to see the truth of those words. There is hardly any joy to equal the joy of giving.

FURTHER STUDY

Deut. 15:7–11;
Matt. 6:1–4;
Phil. 4:10–20

1. What warning does Jesus give?

2. For what does Paul thank the Philippians?

A widow who belonged to a church of which I was the pastor pledged a large amount of money to a certain missionary. It seemed to me that she was being too generous because she had promised to give almost everything she had, and so I attempted to intervene. When I remonstrated with her, however, she burst into tears. 'Would you stop me experiencing the joy of giving and receiving so that I can give again and again?' she asked. I watched in amazement as God worked miracles for her financially so that she was able to give, again and again, until the day she died. My own ministry benefited greatly from her giving. That widow reinforced for me the old saying, that for some might sound like a cliché: you can't out-give God.

One last thing: when you come to make your last will and testament, seek God's guidance. Consider what you will leave to relatives – as they might not use what God has entrusted to you for kingdom purposes – and what you will leave to others.

Lord, help me bring to this task of giving a cheerful and joyful spirit. What I am able to give may be small but in Your hands everything is multiplied. I am so grateful. Amen.

You are special!

FOR READING & MEDITATION – MATTHEW 19:16–30

'love your neighbour as yourself.' (v19)

Another issue we will now explore is how to be free from a sense of inferiority. One writer imagines a child in the womb saying, 'I'm afraid to go out into that strange world. I'm comfortable and secure here. I don't want to be born.' Such fear of life would be extremely debilitating. Many, however, are afraid of life because they are paralysed by a sense of inferiority and do not accept whatever life has to offer them with confidence and joy. A sense of inferiority is real and awful; at its worst it can develop into self-loathing. Sadly, some people's lives are blighted by it even into old age.

FURTHER STUDY

Eph. 1:4–14;
Col. 1:10–14

1. What blessings come to us from being chosen by God?

2. For what does Paul give thanks?

Before we can explore how to gain freedom from inferiority, we must consider its roots. The home and school are often the greenhouse in which the seeds of self-disdain begin to sprout. Parents – even good and kind parents – can, albeit accidently, give a child the idea that they love him or her for something: good marks in exams, proficiency at sport and so on. Parental expectations can put great pressure upon a child unless they are combined with the message, 'We love you for you and not for what you can make of yourself.' When a child feels he or she is not coming up to expectations, self-despising can arise in the heart and that child or young person becomes a secret martyr to inward loathing.

The Bible assumes (as our text for today implies) that healthy souls will have a proper love for themselves. If we regard ourselves as a disappointment and unworthy of love, then it is possible we will come to regard others in the same way. Remember: you may feel inferior in your own sight but you are not inferior in God's sight. He sees you as *special*.

Heavenly Father, deliver me, I pray, from any inner self-despising. May I be prepared to let You come and change my sense of inferiority into one of adequacy. In Jesus' name. Amen.

No sham

FOR READING & MEDITATION – LUKE 9:18–27

'For whoever wants to save his life will lose it, but whoever loses his life for me will save it.' (v24)

Self-loathing, which is often present in attitudes of inferiority, does not always parade itself as self-loathing. It sometimes assumes the manner of superiority. Some who feel inferior may strut and adopt an attitude while others may talk loud and long. Neither possesses the dignity and poise that comes from a well-integrated personality. Dr Alfred Adler, the psychologist who coined the term 'inferiority complex', said, 'Superior attitudes and delusions of grandeur are nothing more than the reverse side of an inferiority complex.' The word psychologists use to describe this is 'compensation'. 'I shall be coming to your church in my Rolls Royce,' wrote a man in a note to me many years ago. Compensation. Inside himself he felt small; inside the Rolls Royce he felt big.

Our text for today tells us that those who try to save their life will succeed only in losing it. The attempt to save one's life by concentrating on it and dressing it up gets a person nowhere. And have you noticed that people who make a lot of noise and parade around, considering themselves superior, are rarely popular? One psychologist expressed this opinion: 'The pose and the noise are calculated to cover self-contempt in the soul.'

A deacon in a church I pastored gave everyone the impression he was full of confidence. Yet in the privacy of a soundproofed counselling room he told me that inwardly he felt small and inferior. 'It's all a cover-up,' he confessed, 'a bid to overcome the littleness I feel on the inside.' Compensation. Those who are not sure of themselves will often bolster themselves up by putting on an outward show. They lack integration. Thank God that He is a marvellous Saviour.

FURTHER STUDY

Psa. 34:1–3;
1 Cor. 1:26–31;
2 Cor. 6:3–10

1. In whom should we boast?

2. How did Paul commend himself?

Lord, may I live my life without any sham. Help me be the person You intend me to be – someone who is healthy in soul and integrated in personality. This I ask in Jesus' name. Amen.

'The light of life'

FOR READING & MEDITATION – PSALM 56:1–13

'For you have delivered me from death ... that I may walk before God in the light of life.' (v13)

I once read of a student who did some research into the various types of people who can be found in a church. After visiting a number of churches, he decided churchgoers fall into one of four groups. The first group, he wrote, 'accept with courage the common lot of mankind, expecting no concessions from life'. The second group comprises 'those who are somewhat personally dislocated or socially maladjusted, or both, but somehow contrive to accept life's second-bests and achieve a measure of satisfaction and joy'. The third group is made up of 'those who are undone, defeated and downcast, and never seem to rise above a spirit of defeatism'. The fourth group consists of 'those who have lost out completely, some of them victims of crimes, some hopeless in chronic invalidism'. If that classification is fair, then all except the first group need help overcoming inferiority and a sense of defeat.

FURTHER STUDY

Prov. 28:13;
Isa. 6:1–7;
Heb. 9:11–14

1. How was Isaiah's sin dealt with?

2. What does Jesus' blood achieve for us?

The Message translation of today's text reads: 'You pulled me from the brink of death, my feet from the cliff-edge of doom. Now I stroll at leisure with God in the sunlit fields of life.' How do we step out of the darkness of inferiority into 'the sunlit fields of life'? First, we must deal with lingering feelings of guilt. It is one thing to have had been freed and forgiven at the time of conversion but it is another to be free from the consequences of sin in our daily lives. If there is some unconfessed sin in your life at the present time then bring it to Jesus. Confess your sin to God and ask for His forgiveness. You can never get on top of things if there is secret unconfessed sin at the base of your life. That produces a central paralysis and inferiority.

Gracious loving and forgiving God, I come to You once again for cleansing and forgiveness. I confess every sin and accept Your loving forgiveness through the blood of Your Son shed on Calvary for me. In His peerless and precious name, I pray. Amen.

His child

FOR READING & MEDITATION – ROMANS 8:1–17

*'Now if we are children, then we are heirs – heirs of God
and co-heirs with Christ' (v17)*

Once we have truly realised we have forgiveness for our sin, the next thing to do to move from inferiority to adequacy is to remind ourselves that, however little worth there may be in us by nature, God put His worth upon us by dying for us on the cross. That truth, gripped by the heart as well as the mind, will begin to bring healing to any self-loathing. God does not love us *for* anything, eg because we are good, clever, industrious or useful to Him. He loves us for ourselves alone. He knows us – really knows us. As we learn to live in the good of this truth transformation takes place.

Frequently I have asked people struggling with a deep sense of inferiority, 'What does being a child of God mean to you?' Usually they give a rationally acceptable answer, but I can tell that the truth has never really gripped them in their hearts. Is that the case with you? Do you just accept the truth or does it grip you with its awesome reality? Listen again: *you are a child of God!* You are as dear to God as His own Son. My words alone cannot get this truth from your head into your heart so I am praying that the Holy Spirit will illuminate it to you as never before.

Grasp this fact also: there is no inferiority or superiority in the Christian scheme of things. The apostle Paul said, 'If the foot should say, "Because I am not a hand, I do not belong to the body," it would not for that reason cease to be part of the body' (1 Cor. 12:15). There are no inferior or superior people in the Christian Church. We are all sinners saved by grace, and every person is dear to God, not because of what he or she does but because of who he or she is – His child.

FURTHER STUDY

Gal. 3:26–4:7;
Eph. 2:13,18–22

1. Who are we in Christ Jesus?

2. Reflect on who we are together in the Lord.

Father, help me see that my life has eternal significance, since I am part of Your Body – eternal plans are being worked out through me. Though I may not be a big cog in the wheel, without me the wheel wouldn't turn. Amen.

No defensiveness

FOR READING & MEDITATION – EPHESIANS 4:1–16

'From him the whole body ... grows and builds itself up in love, as each part does its work.' (v16)

A further thing we can to do to enjoy freedom from inferiority is to approach everything we do – even the most insignificant things – in a significant way. The apostle Paul tells us in today's text that 'each part in its own special way helps the other parts, so that the whole body is healthy and growing and full of love' (TLB). When you perform your part, you enable the whole to function in the way it was designed.

Brother Lawrence, a monk who lived in the seventeenth century, worked for fifteen years in the kitchens of his monastery and said that he did everything for the love of God – the scrubbing of floors, the washing of pans, in fact, every single task. Nothing is insignificant when it is done for the love of God.

Also, be willing to accept advice from others without letting it diminish your sense of worth. When Leonardo da Vinci was painting his famous picture of the Last Supper, one of his friends is said to have remarked that the two cups in the picture were so beautiful that they were the focus of attention. Immediately Leonardo da Vinci painted them out and started again, saying, 'I don't want you to focus on the cups but on the faces.' His willingness to accept correction was what made him a master. When we are on the defensive we are in danger of losing perspective on the important things. Defensive people are rarely growing people; inwardly they remain unchanged. A minister friend of mine received a note from one of his congregation in which this comment was made: 'You keep saying "pronounciation" instead of "pronunciation".' His response? 'Thank you!' His humble spirit saved him from a sense of being either inferior or superior.

FURTHER STUDY

Prov. 15:31–33;
2 Tim. 3:16;
1 Pet. 5:5–7

1. What is Scripture useful for?

2. What do the humble receive?

Father, save me from all defensiveness. Help me accept all advice and correction in the right spirit and see it as a contribution rather than a condemnation. In Jesus' name, I pray. Amen.

'A spring in my step'

FOR READING & MEDITATION – PHILIPPIANS 4:10–20

'I can do everything through him who gives me strength.' (v13)

One last suggestion in this matter of gaining freedom from feelings of inferiority is this: put yourself in God's hands at the start of each day, asking for His strength to help you. God is always ready to turn our bad into good, and make our good better, as long as we make ourselves open and available to His resources.

Once, after I had addressed a group on this subject of inferiority, a man spoke to me and showed me this verse from the prophecy of Micah: 'I will make the lame a remnant, those driven away a strong nation. The LORD will rule over them in Mount Zion from that day and for ever' (Micah 4:7). He said, 'I was plagued with feelings of inferiority and was on the point of suicide when I opened up a Gideon Bible in a hotel room and read these words. I knew God was speaking to me and I took those words to heart. I became a new man and went out into the world feeling neither inferior nor superior. I used to be 'lame', but now I have a spring in my step. Every day when I awake, I put myself at God's disposal, realising that if I am to accomplish everything God intends then His strength must be added to my own. This gives every day a sense of mission and direction. Believe me, no one had a more colossal inferiority complex than I did as a young man.' What changed this man? The sense that his life was being directed by the will of God.

So there it is! If you secretly feel inferior and are inwardly unsure of yourself, look to Jesus who is so whole, so dignified, so completely the Master of every situation. You are His child. You are not inferior, so you need not feel inferior. You are a child of the living God. Pray this prayer written by E. Stanley Jones:

FURTHER STUDY

Col. 1:15–20;
2 Tim. 4:16–18

1. Reflect on the supremacy of Christ.

2. What gave Paul reassurance?

'O God, give me sympathy and sense, and help me keep my courage high. God, give me confidence and strength. And please – a twinkle in my eye.' In Jesus' name. Amen.

'Grief work'

FOR READING & MEDITATION – 1 THESSALONIANS 4:13–18

'we do not want you to be ignorant about those who fall asleep, or to grieve like the rest of men, who have no hope.' (v13)

Now we move on to an issue that may not affect everyone, but my experience has shown that more struggle with this than we might realise. I refer to the matter of excessive grief or loss. Please note that this is about *excessive grief* – as grief is absolutely natural. It comes to us all, as it is an essential ingredient of being human. However, when grief is excessive or extended over many years, this is when further complications may occur.

Almost everyone reading these lines will have lost a loved one. It may be that you are in the throes of grief at this very moment as, through illness or an accident, someone very close to you has been taken away. As difficult as it may be, please don't try to subdue the process of grieving. It is a natural part of life – as natural as crying when you experience sudden, severe physical pain. Even Jesus wept at the grave of a loved one (see John 11:35). We grieve, said Paul in our text today, but not like the rest of men who have no hope. Alfred Tennyson wrote in *The Ancient Sage*:

My son, the world is dark with griefs and graves,
So dark that men cry out against the heavens.

FURTHER STUDY

2 Sam. 1:17–2:7;
John 11:32–36

1. How did David react to the deaths of Saul and Jonathan?

2. How did Jesus react to the death of Lazarus?

Since grief is part of our lot on this earth it is helpful to learn something of its nature and how to navigate it. People have often talked about 'grief work', meaning we have to be willing to work through our grief if we are to find healing for the soul. Those who try to avoid grief will find that the escape routes are all cul-de-sacs – dead ends. For many, grief may seem like a prison, but let's take steps to ensure that we do not stay longer in it than we should. Grief is to be faced, but it need not be nursed.

Father, I see that it is helpful and natural to grieve when a loved one dies, but please help me so that sorrow does not sour me. Give me grace to handle all things in life in a godly way. In Jesus' name. Amen.

Coming to terms with grief

FOR READING & MEDITATION – PSALM 88:1–18

'my eyes are dim with grief.' (v9)

The writer C.S. Lewis describes in *A Grief Observed* the devastation he felt when his wife, Joy, died of cancer. His openness has encouraged many, over the years, caught in the throes of grief. So overwhelmed was he by grief that God seemed far away. In an honest but frank mood he wrote, 'Go to Him when your need is desperate, when all other help is in vain, and what do you find? A door slammed in your face.' He was careful to point out that that was how he felt; it was not the reality. At a later stage he wrote, 'Grief is like a long winding valley … sometimes you are presented with exactly the same sort of country you thought you had left behind miles ago.' Eventually Lewis recovered from his inconsolable grief and described the process: 'There was no sudden striking and emotional transition. It was like the warming of a room or the coming of daylight.'

FURTHER STUDY

Job 1:18–22;
Isa. 53:3–5;
1 Pet. 2:21–25

1. How did Job come to terms with his grief?

2. Whose sins and sorrows did Jesus bear?

How can we allow this God-given process space to take place without crippling us for years? First, accept that the loss of a loved one *will* result in grief and sadness. This will save you from thinking you have been singled out for unfair treatment. It may be possible to prepare yourself for grief by telling yourself, 'Grief is the lot of everyone on this earth and I am no exception.' I am not suggesting you adopt this attitude in a morbid way; simply come to terms with the truth and then forget it. If you do this, if and when the wave of grief crashes over your life, you will be less likely to respond to the situation with aggrieved self-pity. The idea that you are being singled out for harsh treatment brings further complications and inhibits recovery and healing.

Lord Jesus, I am so glad that You know grief and loss, for indeed all our griefs are Yours. You take them into Your heart. Help me to share my griefs with You for I know that a grief shared is a grief halved. In Your name. Amen.

Not 'around' but 'through'

FOR READING & MEDITATION – LUKE 4:14–30

'But he walked right through the crowd and went on his way.' (v30)

Yesterday we saw that the first step in dealing with grief is to accept it will come to us all. Secondly, don't try to escape grief through illusions or subterfuges. Sometimes these can be worse than the grief itself. I have met many Christians who have been unwilling to grieve over the loss of a loved one because they consider it to be unchristian.*

I have chosen today's reading to highlight to you that when Jesus was faced with a crisis He did not back off or try to escape. He went straight 'through'. The Christian way is always 'through' an issue. One woman who refused to grieve after the loss of her daughter on the grounds that it was 'unspiritual', was admitted to hospital some months later with a twisted bowel. Her doctor commented, 'She may have avoided this if she had been willing to grieve.' You may have thought C.S. Lewis' reaction to his wife's death, to which we referred yesterday, was unspiritual, but he honestly faced the reality of what was going on in his soul. It's better by far to be honest than to pretend something is better than it is – a common problem with many Christians. God desires truth in the inward parts (Psa. 51:6).

FURTHER STUDY

Psa. 31:1–10;
31:14–22;
Mark 14:32–36

1. How did David pray in a time of crisis?

2. How did Jesus pray in a time of crisis?

Most importantly, share your grief with Jesus. Don't try and carry it without Him. Prayer helps, even though your prayer may at first be a complaint. Jeremiah once started his prayer with a complaint, 'O LORD, you deceived me' but went on to say, 'his word is in my heart like a fire' (Jer. 20:7,9). God would much prefer you to tell Him exactly how you feel than to pretend things are other than they are. Remember this: God understands you completely, whether or not you realise it.

Father, save me from all pretence. Help me to be open and honest about my feelings and to put everything into Your hands – even my complaints. In Jesus' name, I pray. Amen.

*For further reading on the topic of grief and loss, try *Insight into Bereavement* (CWR, 2006).

CWR

Helping you live life God's way

...through gaining insight into life's issues

CWR's Insight books and courses have been developed in response to the needs that many people have to understand and face key life issues such as depression, self-esteem, addiction, perfectionism and anxiety.

Offering biblical teaching on a range of issues, the books and day courses provide practical insight for both those who want to help others and those who face these issues themselves.

'The course helped me understand what I went through and will help me help others.'

For further details on upcoming Insight Days and for the full range of books in the *Waverley Abbey Insight Series* visit, **www.cwr.org.uk/insight**

You can also discover our wide variety of short courses, seminars and events, which cover many different topics from discipleship to pastoral care, at **www.cwr.org.uk/courses**

Immutity to devastation

FOR READING & MEDITATION – JOB 23:1–12

'I have treasured the words of his mouth more than my daily bread.'
(v12)

One of the best ways of coping with grief is to regularly expose yourself to the truths contained in God's Word. A woman once told me that she had been a reader of *Every Day with Jesus* for twenty years, and when her husband died she felt deeply distraught but not devastated. 'When I knew he was dying,' she said, 'I wondered how I could cope. I was surprised at the way scriptural truths kept coming to my mind, each one bringing a wave of healing with it, and I realised that my daily dipping into the Bible had built within me an immunity to devastation.'

FURTHER STUDY

Deut. 8:1–3;
Neh. 8:18–9:3;
Matt. 4:1–11

1. How did the Israelites strengthen themselves in days of pain?

2. How did Jesus face up to a time of trial?

I could identify with this woman, as I too have grieved. Some years ago, as many of you will know, my wife died of cancer, and within three weeks of her death my father died of a heart attack. Then I lost my only sons, David and John – John to a liver disease and David, just ten months later, as the result of a massive heart attack. In an interview I was asked, 'Did you ever ask God "Why?"' I considered this and said, 'No, I never once asked "Why?"' My answer started a train of thought in my mind and I wondered 'Why didn't you ever ask "Why?"?' It dawned on me that hours spent soaking myself in Scripture had built within me a certain immunity. Did I cry when my loved ones died? Yes. Was I distraught? Yes. Was I devastated? No. Please don't interpret this as an attempt to be spiritually superior, but I can honestly say the question in my heart was not 'Why?' but 'How can God use my pain to help others who are in pain?' This response could only be the consequence of the ingesting and digesting of Scripture. The Word does indeed build immunity to devastation.

Father, I see that the daily intake of Your Word into my soul builds an immunity against devastation. May I be like Job, who treasured Your words more than his daily bread. In Jesus' name. Amen.

Comfort through contribution

FOR READING & MEDITATION – 2 CORINTHIANS 1:1–11

*'God ... comforts us in all our troubles, so that we can comfort those
in any trouble' (vv3–4)*

We have been discussing how to process grief and we now consider what I believe to be the best way to guard against excessive and prolonged grief: ask God to help you use your pain to heal the pain of others. Meister Eckhart, a fourteenth-century German Dominican theologian, wrote, 'God's every affliction is a lure – a lure to help you help others.' You are made tender by your sorrow, and that tenderness, if offered to God, can make your service far more effective and powerful.

People who have read my writings for years told me that after my wife died in 1986 they noticed a difference in my approach. Whereas before I had been very matter of fact, since her death there has been a greater sensitivity to people's struggles in life and a desire to get alongside them rather than browbeat them into submission to God's commands. I am well aware of this increased sensitivity to the struggles people have and constantly thank God for it.

One man whose son was murdered spent time carefully processing his grief before God. After prayer one day he got up and said, 'Lord, I have grieved long enough. What have You for me to do?' He was prompted to look at the news and newspapers for reports of those who had been murdered and write to their loved ones offering help and support. Far more people are murdered in Britain each year than is generally realised, since many cases never make the national news or headlines. This man finds that the contribution he makes brings him increasing strength. I was deeply struck by what he said when I spoke to him about this. 'I found I could give most,' he said, 'when most had been taken away.'

FURTHER STUDY

Isa. 40:1–9, 27–31;
1 Thess. 5:4–11

1. What comfort does the prophet give God's people?

2. What does Paul suggest we give each other?

Lord God, grant that whenever I have to face grief I shall take the comfort You give me and pass it on to others. Help me not to just bear my grief but allow You to use it for Your glory. In Jesus' name. Amen.

A new heredity

FOR READING & MEDITATION – 2 CORINTHIANS 5:11–21

*'Therefore, if anyone is in Christ, he is a new creation;
the old has gone, the new has come!' (v17)*

Another matter that we need God's help to be free from is the influence of our past. We touched a little on this when we discussed the subject of inferiority, but over the next few days I would like us to think about it in greater detail. Can we claim the restoration of God to overcome influences from childhood that have had a negative effect upon us? Some say we can't. One psychiatrist writes, 'We can never get away from the negative influences we experienced in childhood. We must learn to live within our limitations.'

FURTHER STUDY

John 1:10–13;
1 Pet. 1:3,23–25

1. What is given to those who receive Jesus?

2. Through what means have we been born again?

During a meeting of Christians at which this issue was being discussed, a woman asked, 'Should I think of the negative aspects of my early emotional conditioning, which have been reinforced by over forty years of living, as something that can be overcome or do I just modify their effect a little?' The group leader answered, 'What you were you are, and you have to do the best you can with the material you have been given.' Was he right? My experience has shown that this need not be the case. I have seen many people affected by the powerful, cleansing, remaking love of God to such a degree that they have overcome the negative influences of childhood. The new life cancelled out the old life. Though some may question it, the possibility is there.

A man whose childhood was traumatic once stood up in a meeting at which I was present and told those gathered there, 'I am a witness to the fact that God does "restore the years that the locusts have eaten". Christ has reconditioned me.' As I was this man's counsellor, I was aware of the details of his story and knew that what he was saying was true. In Jesus we have a new heredity.

Gracious Father, I am so thankful that, whatever the environment in which I was brought up, I have new life in You. Help me not just to realise this but apply the truth to my life. In Jesus' name. Amen.

Nothing final but God

FOR READING & MEDITATION – EZEKIEL 36:22–28

'I will give you a new heart and put a new spirit in you' (v26)

One of the most mature Christians I have ever known was brought up in a home where both parents were alcoholics. He was the youngest of six boys – and his five older brothers landed up in prison. As the youngest, he was put on not only by his parents but by his brothers too. When the parents beat the older brothers they, in turn, took it out on him.

As a teenager, he went into a church one Sunday morning for the purpose of 'casing the joint' to see if there was anything he could steal. He listened intently as a young man stood at the front and told of his conversion to Jesus and how his life had been changed. An evangelistic invitation was given, and my friend walked to the front and surrendered his life to Jesus. The change in him was remarkable. From the very moment he breathed in the new air of the kingdom he became radically different. People who knew him and his environment said, 'I would never have believed it unless I had seen it.' So powerful was the transformation that he became a pillar of the community and was elected mayor of his town. At his institution service I had the joy of giving the mayoral address. I took as my text the words we thought about yesterday: 'if anyone is in Christ, he is a new creation'.

Our early emotional environment is not final: it can be redeemed and restored – even cancelled. We may have been brought up in challenging and difficult circumstances but all of us have the privilege of a new birth and environment in Jesus. Horizontal influences may have corrupted us but, given our consent and co-operation, the vertical influences can cleanse and convert. Nothing is final, but God.

FURTHER STUDY

Joel 2:25–32;
John 3:1–8;
Acts 2:36–41

1. What promises are made to those who call on the Lord?

2. What promise is for all who accept Jesus?

Father, I am so grateful that nothing is final but You. And I belong to Your kingdom. Therefore I am a candidate for being made over again. Thank You, my Father. Amen.

Growing into Christ's image

FOR READING & MEDITATION – 2 PETER 1:1–11

'he has given us his very great and precious promises, so that through them you may participate in the divine nature' (v4)

Today's reading reveals to us that when we belong to Jesus we 'participate in the divine nature' – we have a new heredity. The new can cancel out the old, if we are willing.

During a visit to India, some friends who were transporting me to a meeting began to talk about the change that Jesus makes in our lives when we surrender to Him. They told me about a man they knew was from a tribe that was looked down upon by every other in India. A sense of inferiority was in every breath he breathed when he was a boy.

Someone, however, gave him the good news about Jesus and he became a Christian. Within a year or two, as a result of his Christlike character, he had become a powerful influence in the community, winning hundreds to the Saviour. He married and had six children, every one of whom became a college graduate. In his home, I understand, there is an amazing sense of peace. So great is the change in this man that people find it difficult to reconcile his present with his past.

Many other illustrations of people overcoming deprived and difficult early environments spring to mind. I once visited a man in prison who had been converted to Jesus through the witness of one of the inmates. He told me a story of rejection, abuse and emotional deprivation in his early life such as I have never heard before. I wondered just how he would recover from all this. After leaving prison, however, he joined a church and found a job. Eventually he got married and trained to be a counsellor. Now he is one of the finest counsellors I know. The wounds in his soul have all been healed. His new heredity shines through.

FURTHER STUDY

2 Cor. 6:16–7:1;
Phil. 1:4–6;
1 Pet. 1:18–19

1. How does God describe His relationship with us?

2. From what are we redeemed, according to Peter?

Father, how can I ever thank You sufficiently for making me a participant in 'the divine nature'? Help me grow and transform day by day into the image of Your Son. In His precious name, I pray. Amen.

Helping you live life God's way

...through personal transformation

God is able to bring about transformation in *all* of us – no matter what. CWR's books such as Brian Greenaway's real-life story, *The Monster Within*, have inspired and helped transform many readers' lives...

❝ *Your book was the final sign I needed to change my life to help change others.* ❞

❝ *I read this book and a weight lifted off me. I came to the realisation that if God loves me now then I don't have to be alone. I felt like I never wanted to change prior to this ... I cried for the first time in ten years and was left with an immense feeling of calmness.* ❞

All our Bible-based books and resources enable people to experience personal transformation through applying God's Word to their lives and relationships. To find out more, visit **www.cwr.org.uk**

The divine exchange

FOR READING & MEDITATION – GALATIANS 2:11–21

*'I have been crucified with Christ and I no longer live,
but Christ lives in me.' (v20)*

I wonder how you feel about the issue we are exploring at the moment – overcoming childhood environment and influence. Perhaps you are saying to yourself, 'Even though I am a Christian I am still affected by what happened in my childhood. I feel as if the inner child of the past has not only survived but has thrived. I have grown up on the outside but not on the inside.' If that is so, how do you resolve the situation? How do you gain freedom from it?

First, let me take you back to something said yesterday: when we belong to Jesus we 'participate in the divine nature' – we have a new heredity. The new can cancel out the old, if we are willing. There's the rub: *if we are willing.* Martin Luther used to talk about 'the divine exchange'. As far as I can tell, this is what he meant: the more we give ourselves to God the more He gives Himself to us. If we give only a little of ourselves to Him then He is able to give only a little of Himself to us.

Why is it, I have asked myself a thousand times, that some Christians advance more in a year than others do in a lifetime? The answer, I think, is that our growth as Christians is governed by how much of ourselves we are prepared to entrust to Jesus and the Holy Spirit. My experience of dealing with people and my understanding of God's Word have convinced me that when we open ourselves to Jesus, a work can be done in our hearts that releases the pull and negative influences of previous years. It all depends, of course, on how much we are willing to trust Him. We have full access to our Father God. Of that there is no doubt. The question we must answer is: Does He have full access to us?

FURTHER STUDY

Rom. 5:9–11;
James 4:7–10

1. Meditate on the 'how much more' spoken of by Paul.

2. What happens when we come near to God?

Father, I want You to have all there is of me. Forgive me that I draw back from opening up the whole of my life to You. I am making the decision to change that – today. In Jesus' name. Amen.

The hour of decision

SAT
11 FEB

FOR READING & MEDITATION – 1 CORINTHIANS 13:1–13

*'When I was a child, I talked like a child, I thought like a child …
When I became a man, I put childish ways behind me.' (v11)*

Assuming that you are willing to give yourself wholeheartedly to Jesus, what comes next in the quest to find freedom from negative childhood environments and influences? Remember it is not self-mastery we are talking about here, but teaming up with God so that we receive and draw on His resources and do not rely on our own. Another principle is based on something Paul mentions in the chapter we have read today. He tells us that when he was a child he talked like a child, thought like a child, reasoned like a child, but when he became a man he put childish ways behind him. The Greek word he uses here to indicate the putting away of childish things – *katargeo* – means 'to render inoperative'. He used that word to indicate that he had made a clear decision to have done with childish things.

FURTHER STUDY

Matt. 7:7–12;
Titus 2:11–14;
3:1–8

1. What encouragement does Jesus give to those who ask?

2. What difference do God's love and grace make in our lives?

When seeking to be free of negative emotional influences from childhood, it is good to see the issue as one that needs to be dealt with, and then to enlist God's help. The apostle James tells us that often the reason why we don't receive is that we don't ask (James 4:2). If early emotional influences have left you with wounds, then ask God to render their influences inoperative.

Many years ago, I sat with a seventy-year-old man who wept as he admitted the whole of his life had been plagued with memories of a bad childhood. 'Have you ever asked God to deliver you from them?' I asked. 'No,' he replied, 'I have never seen them as something I ought to bring to God.' 'Shall we do so now?' I suggested. God did something very powerful in that man's life. If you, too, are struggling, He can do the same for you.

Father, help me to receive Your help in overcoming negative childhood influences and to let the new work that You have begun reach every part of me. I wait before You. May Your power be at work this very hour. Amen.

Removing the bonds

FOR READING & MEDITATION – JOHN 11:38–44

'Jesus said to them, "Take off the grave clothes and let him go."' (v44)

Hopefully some will benefit from what I have said over the past few days about bad childhood influences, but others will not. This is not because the suggestions work only for some and not others, but because a number of people will need to sit down with a counsellor and talk matters through in much greater depth. In the past, people have accused me of giving simplistic solutions to complex problems. I have to trust that the Holy Spirit will use my few words in this contained space and cause them to wing their way into people's hearts (and often He does), but as a counsellor I know that some issues have to be talked through with a godly person before the light begins to dawn.

FURTHER STUDY

Mark 5:1–9,15, 18–20;
Col. 3:5–14

1. What effect did Jesus' deliverance have on Legion?

2. What are we to put off and put on?

In today's reading, notice what happened when Jesus brought Lazarus back from the dead. Jesus gave him life but then He turned to those around Him and bid them remove the strips of cloth from Lazarus' body. Though the Lord gave Lazarus life, He invited others to give him liberty in life.

A Christian brother said to me on one occasion, 'I'm Irish, you know, and I have a flaming temper. My father had a temper and his father before him. It's hereditary.' 'But you have a new Father,' I said, 'and therefore the possibility of a new heredity. Let's talk about this new heredity that has temper left out.' We talked at great length, resulting in him surrendering his whole being to God, allowing the new heredity to take over.

If you need further help with what I have been saying over the past few days, then why not get that help from a godly counsellor or pastor? You may be so bound up that you need the help of others to remove the bonds that are preventing you from being free.

Father, may I allow this new heredity to transform my life. But, if necessary, may I be prepared to seek the help of others. I long to walk in freedom – freedom from all bondage. Guide me from here onwards. In Jesus' name. Amen.

CWR

Helping you live life God's way

...through counselling and people helping

It is likely that many of us will come into contact with people who are hurting and could benefit from professional counselling. People helping has always been at the very heart of CWR's ministry and, as a result, Waverley Abbey College exists to deliver Higher Education counselling programmes that are underpinned by a Christian world-view.

This has been an inspirational and life-changing programme. Academically deep but relationally dynamic.

If you know someone who would benefit from talking with a counsellor, or want to talk with someone yourself, please visit our Find a Counsellor page on our website to find a Waverley Abbey College trained counsellor in your local area. Or, if you would like to pursue or find out more about counselling training, come to one of our free Open Days. For more information, visit **www.waverleyabbeycollege.ac.uk**

WAVERLEY ABBEY
COLLEGE

The educational
arm of CWR

Advice for the young

FOR READING & MEDITATION – ECCLESIASTES 12:1–8

'Remember your Creator in the days of your youth, before the days of trouble come' (v1)

As we have been looking at childhood influences, I now want to take a few days out to reflect on how we can have freedom to enjoy *whichever* stage of life we are at, whether youth or what is described by some psychologists as the third and fourth age. Each of these periods brings its own challenges and many are not able to adjust to the process of change. Some people never really pass through the different stages of maturity that the years are supposed to bring. They carry over their 'Peter Pan' mentality into the later stages of life, always sighing to be young again. And some who are young refuse to look ahead and prepare. To experience freedom as we pass through the various stages of life, we need to understand that each period is peculiar to itself and has great possibilities.

FURTHER STUDY

Prov. 1:1–9;
1 Tim. 4:7–16

1. How will the young gain knowledge and discretion?

2. How does Paul advise Timothy?

To the young I would like to pass on these words of advice. (1) Realise you are an awakening personality and take as much interest in the development of your soul as your physical development. The most important thing in life is character, and Jesus is the master architect of character. Cleverness may get you to the top but only character will keep you there. (2) Find a cause to which you can give yourself wholeheartedly. Ask God to lay a burden on your heart for a cause that fits your abilities. It could be working with youngsters with learning difficulties, visiting elderly people or helping the homeless. Whatever you do, serve somebody if you are to be a healthy personality, as Jesus Himself did (Matt. 20:28). (3) Set clear goals for yourself – don't drift. Some people allow circumstances or friends to dictate what they do in life. Don't react – act.

Dear God my Father, may I pass through each stage of my life knowing Your guiding and protective hand is upon me. And grant that when I come to the end of my days there will be no useless regrets. In Jesus' name. Amen.

A few more steps

TUES
14 FEB

FOR READING & MEDITATION – ECCLESIASTES 11:7–10

'Be happy, young man, while you are young, and let your heart give you joy in the days of your youth.' (v9)

We continue our suggestions for the first and second ages, although this is good advice for any age. (4) Do the little things well and God will give you bigger opportunities. Remember these words: 'You have been faithful in handling this small amount,' he told him, 'so now I will give you many more responsibilities' (Matt. 25:21, TLB). Many a person has not pushed on in their faith because he or she has fallen and stumbled when dealing with the lesser things.

(5) If you feel marriage is for you, pray about your choice of a life partner. Base your choice on something more than physical attraction. Godliness ought to figure high on your list. Ask yourself: Will I still be in love with this person when sexual desire has diminished? (6) Don't aim for leadership but concentrate on being a servant. 'Whoever wants to become great among you must be your servant,' said Jesus (Mark 10:43). If God wants you to be a leader then He will make you one, but remember, the best leaders come from the best servants. (7) Begin every day by committing its affairs to God. Take time to pray and read the Scriptures.

(8) Learn the benefits of discipline. A disciple is someone who is disciplined. You may have to delay and wait for some things, but the wait will build character into you and develop trust in God. (9) Respect those who are older than you; seek, listen and weigh their advice. (10) Don't be impatient if you can't produce change overnight. Perseverance also helps to build character. And remember, character is the big word in God's economy. Concentrate on being *who* God wants you to be and God will place you *where* He wants you to be.

FURTHER STUDY

1 Tim. 6:11–16, 20–21;
2 Tim. 2:22–26;
1 Pet. 5:5–11

1. Reflect on Paul's charge to Timothy.

2. What counsel does Peter give young men?

Father, I see that if I am not to fail in this business of living then I need You to walk with me hand in hand down the years. May I depend upon Your strength, rely on Your power. In Jesus' name. Amen.

Life to the full

FOR READING & MEDITATION – 1 CORINTHIANS 4:1–16

'in Christ Jesus I became your father through the gospel.
Therefore I urge you to imitate me.' (vv15–16)

Having considered a number of suggestions for overcoming the challenges of the first and second stages, we now consider the third and fourth phases. (1) Don't settle down. Someone said, 'If heaven lies about us in our infancy, then the world lies about us in middle age.' Be careful: you can all to easily become preoccupied with the cares of the world – money, children, career – in this period of life. George Bernard Shaw said that most people could have as their epitaph, 'Died at forty; buried at sixty.' It's at this time when people tend to settle down – and stagnate. Overcome inertia by prayerfully establishing new goals; then go for them.

FURTHER STUDY

Eccl. 12:9–14;
1 Tim. 3:1–10;
Titus 1:6–9;
2:6–8,11–14

1. What conclusion does the writer of Ecclesiastes come to?

2. What should Titus teach?

(2) Where possible, keep physically healthy. We are both physical and spiritual beings, so make an effort to keep fit and not let things go. (3) Be alert to the matter of relationships. Many are drawn into and get entangled in affairs and unhealthy relationships in an attempt to recapture feelings they find are waning. The desire to be attractive to someone, looking for affirmation and recognition especially when you might feel your partner is not attracted to you in the way he or she once was, can lead to great pitfalls.

(4) Be sure, if you are married and have children, to have some interests outside your home – a worthwhile project, for example. This ensures that the focus of your family is on serving others. It will help teach your children to follow in similar ways, and will give you a sense of purpose once they have left home too. Enrol on a course and educate yourself in a subject that will enable you to be of some service to others if necessary. Serve someone else, as Jesus did.

Father, I realise that as I move along in life I am gathering experience. Help me to translate that larger experience into fuller expression. May I grow in usefulness and love. For Jesus' sake. Amen.

'You're looking very well'

FOR READING & MEDITATION – ISAIAH 46:1–7

*'Even to your old age and grey hairs I am he,
I am he who will sustain you.' (v4)*

Someone once described the various life stages as: youth, middle age and 'You're looking very well!' Here are a few more suggestions for those in their third and fourth phases of life. (1) Accept the fact that you are getting older. You can't be fifty any longer, but you can make seventy or eighty or any other decade just as profitable. Each age brings its own rewards and older age brings knowledge that can be put into good effect.

(2) Keep busy. Dr Martin Gumpert, in his book *You are Younger than You Think* (now out of print), said that: 'Idleness is the greatest enemy of the aged and presents them with their ticket to death'. When I was seventy, I was sent a list of people who had accomplished great things after they had reached the appointed three score years and ten. Did you know Michelangelo was painting and designing buildings up to the time of his death at eighty-nine? Many famous people did not even start to make an impact on the world until they were in their middle or older years. (3) Don't try to control your children and interfere in their lives. Be available for advice but give it only when it is asked for. Uninvited interference is one of the biggest causes of irritation between children and their parents.

(4) If you have lost your life partner, work through your grief well but don't allow the rest of your days to be filled with it. If this is an issue for you, go back and re-read what was written earlier concerning excessive grief. (5) Above everything else keep close to God and, if it helps, allow *Every Day with Jesus* to minister to you. Everyone grows older day by day but sadly not everyone grows old gracefully. Be one who does.

FURTHER STUDY

Psa. 91:14–16;
92:12–15;
2 Pet. 3:18

1. What is the testimony of the psalmist?

2. Make Peter's exhortation your prayer.

Father God, help me to grow old gracefully, beautifully and creatively. Please enable me to bring forth fruit even in my old age. May I remain close to You so that old age will not be a sigh but a song. In Jesus' name. Amen.

Stop fighting

FOR READING & MEDITATION – 2 TIMOTHY 3:1–9
'People will be lovers of themselves' (v2)

The struggle to which we turn now is that of self-centredness. Can we experience divine freedom here? Certainly. But first let's understand the depth of the problem. As long as we make ourselves the centre of the universe nothing in our lives will be right, for we are not the centre of the universe – God is. Our text speaks of people being 'lovers of themselves'. This is completely different from the healthy love of self that we talked about. To love yourself is healthy, providing you love your neighbour as yourself, but to be a lover of yourself suggests you love no one but yourself.

FURTHER STUDY

2 Chron. 20:4–13,15; Eph. 6:10–18

1. What made Jehoshaphat so confident?

2. Put on the full armour of God as you pray.

Some people, when they realise they have a problem with egocentricity, attempt to fight it in their own strength. One man who came to CWR's training centre at Waverley Abbey House told the group with whom he was working, 'I have come here to declare a war on myself. I am an egotist and I want to beat this problem before I leave this place.' What he said sounded praiseworthy, but the group helped him understand that really he was powerless to fight himself and that he needed the help of Jesus. I am glad to say he came to see that what the group said was true. He enlisted the aid of Jesus in his struggle with egocentricity and left a changed man. The self needs to surrender to the One who said, 'All authority in heaven and on earth has been given to me' (Matt. 28:18).

A woman who has been reading *Every Day with Jesus* for years commented, 'I notice there is hardly an edition in which you do not use the word "surrender".' This is primarily because I see so many Christians trying to fight life's battles in their own strength.

Father, help me not to declare a full-scale war on myself but to enlist Your aid in the battle for freedom. May I be a truly surrendered person. In Jesus' name, I pray. Amen.

The perfectionist's disease

FOR READING & MEDITATION – 2 THESSALONIANS 3:6–15

*'We hear that some among you are idle. They are not busy;
they are busybodies.' (v11)*

Today we look at some of the symptoms or consequences of self-centredness. Perfectionism is one. Many people who are attempting to deal with this issue try to make themselves perfect. They hope this will resolve the problem of self-esteem, but it doesn't work.

When I studied psychology, I read about a girl whose goal in life was to be perfect. To begin with she had lots of friends, but one by one they fell away. The girl wondered why, then discovered that her friends realised she was not interested in them but only in herself and her perfectionism. Not only did she lose her friends but she also lost her own self-esteem and came to loathe herself. An unusual outcome, you might think – a girl who wanted to be perfect ending up loathing herself. But since her basic premise was flawed, she would never feel perfect. She made herself the centre of her universe and broke an important law of life: to find your life you must lose it.

Another consequence of self-centredness is attempting to make other people perfect. People who try to change everyone around them and make *them* perfect are experienced by those around them as 'busybodies'. They busy themselves by dominating others and wanting to change them. Karl Menninger, an American psychiatrist, said, 'I see several times a month what may be called the fuss-budget's or the perfectionist's disease. It is the disease that fastens itself upon a woman or man who wants everything just so around the house and the office. And it tends to grow worse as the person grows older.' Do you like to control people and impose your will on others? Then be careful; you may be setting yourself up for a fall.

FURTHER STUDY

Mark 10:35–45;
1 Cor. 3:4,18–23

1. What does Jesus teach His disciples about greatness?

2. What superior attitude does Paul expose?

God my Father, pull off the mask that hides my self from myself, and may I be prepared to stand before You as I am, warts and all. Bring everything that is not of You out into the open. In Jesus' name, I pray. Amen.

The Word

FOR READING & MEDITATION – 1 JOHN 3:1–10

'How great is the love the Father has lavished on us, that we should be called children of God!' (v1)

The unsurrendered self can disguise itself in many forms. One of the things I have discovered in dealing with people over many years is that those who can't get their way can, in extreme situations, sometimes retreat into ill health. If they can't get attention one way, they will get it another.

The American writer and lecturer Dale Carnegie once spoke of a bright, vigorous girl who became unwell in order to feel important. One day she realised that she was getting on in age and was not married. The lonely years stretched out ahead of her, so she took to her bed with a mysterious condition. For ten years her mother cared for her by nursing her, carrying her food to her and doing everything that was needed. Then one day the mother, weary of service, lay down and died. After the funeral the daughter, realising there was no one to look after her, got up out of bed and resumed living again. John Dewey, a one-time Senator in the USA, has commented, 'The deepest urge is the desire to be important. And if illness makes us feel important, we take to illness.'

FURTHER STUDY

Acts 8:9–22;
Col. 2:16–19

1. How did Peter react to Simon?

2. Where is reality found?

Sometimes a driven self makes us try to 'add a cubit to our height', so to speak, by putting undue emphasis on titles. There is nothing wrong with having a title, but it is very dangerous to find your significance in a title. We can only find our significance in who we are in God, not in what we do. Catherine the Great, I learned while studying her life, would never open a letter unless it was addressed to 'Her Imperial Majesty'. And yet this is what the angel told Joseph before Jesus was born: 'You are to give him the name Jesus' (Matt. 1:21). Not a title but just one word – Jesus. But that one word has become the Word.

Lord God, save me from myself. May I not attempt to add a cubit to my height in order to make myself feel more significant. Show me how to be myself – in You. For Jesus' sake. Amen.

The last thing to go

MON
20 FEB

FOR READING & MEDITATION – LUKE 14:25–35

*'If anyone comes to me and does not hate his father and mother ...
yes, even his own life – he cannot be my disciple.' (v26)*

The last thing we want to do is to let go of ourselves. We will let go of other things more easily. But our self-interest and nature? This is where the real struggle takes place.

As you read today's reading did you notice that Jesus insists we are to give up the self if we are to be His disciples? Here is His message again: 'If anyone comes to me and does not hate his father and mother, his wife and children, his brothers and sisters – yes, even his own life – he cannot be my disciple.' By the way, to 'hate' does not mean to feel hostility; a comparison with other statements Jesus made reveals it means 'to love less'. The Living Bible uses this wording: 'Anyone who wants to be my follower must love me far more than he does his own father, mother ... otherwise he cannot be my disciple.' One commentator said: 'A lighted candle, when it is put before a high-powered electric light, casts a shadow. Thus the lesser loves, while really light, cast a shadow when this all-consuming Love makes a demand upon the human spirit. These loves are not to be abandoned; they are to be surrendered.'

It's interesting, isn't it, that the 'life', or our old selfish nature, is the last thing Jesus mentions. Is it because the self – or our 'life' – is the last thing we are willing to give up? A missionary once told me that he gave up his home, his family and a good job to go to the mission field but when he got there he realised that he hadn't given himself up. He made this discovery when he found himself getting touchy about matters such as position and power. 'The real battle in life,' someone has remarked, 'is over what we do with the self; all other things are skirmishes.' I agree.

FURTHER STUDY

Dan. 4:28–37;
Phil. 3:1–10

1. What lesson did Nebuchadnezzar learn?

2. What had the apostle Paul given up?

Heavenly Father, I come to You afresh for Your help in this vital matter. I confess I find it difficult to let go of this last thing, but I am willing to be made willing. Help me my Father. In Jesus' name. Amen.

Challenged to be changed

FOR READING & MEDITATION – ROMANS 6:1–14

'For we know that our old self was crucified with him so that the body of sin might be done away with' (v6)

As we have already acknowledged, we cannot fight our selfish nature. For this reason we remind ourselves that it is not self-mastery that we are seeking but God-given freedom. Before we move on to resolutions let us ask ourselves: Why do we lie and steal? We think we will be advantaged or protected. Why do we quarrel with others? Because somebody has got in our way. Why are we jealous or envious of others? Because we are afraid that they will get ahead of us. The psychologist Dr Alfred Adler was right when he said that the ego urge is our prime difficulty in life and is at the root of most of our unhappiness.

FURTHER STUDY

Rom. 13:11–14; Gal. 5:19–26

1. What does Paul call 'deeds of darkness'?

2. What does he call 'the fruit of the Spirit'?

So what's the answer? Here it is again: *surrender*. The key to dealing with our self-centred nature is surrender. 'But didn't I do that at conversion?' you might say. Yes, you did in a measure, but probably not wholly. Your conscious mind was given to Jesus at conversion and now there is need to lay your subconscious mind before Him. Our basic motivation can be cleansed, renewed and redeemed and this happens as we surrender more completely to Him.

Trusting God is not always easy. We might react as Simon Peter did when Jesus predicted His death and say, 'Never, Lord. Don't talk about crucifixion. It's too distasteful to even think about' (Matt. 16:22, paraphrased). There is a constant struggle between our sinful nature and the Holy Spirit (see Rom. 7:7–25), and we must always be aware of this. However, as our text for today tells us, our old self was crucified with Jesus and it is powerless to enslave us to sin. It may give up a good fight at times, but we *can* say no to sin and be changed through the power of the Holy Spirit.

Father, I am so thankful that I need not be a slave to sin. Once I was in slavery but Your death on the cross has set me free. Help me live forever in that freedom. In Jesus' name, I pray. Amen.

Next Issue

MAR/APR 2017

The Call

When Jesus first called to the disciples, they would have had no idea of the amazing, life-changing, roller-coaster journey ahead.

During this Easter season, Selwyn unpacks what it means to respond to Jesus' call. Explore how Jesus lived, taught and shared His life with His disciples, experiencing together both the cost and the crown of responding to His call.

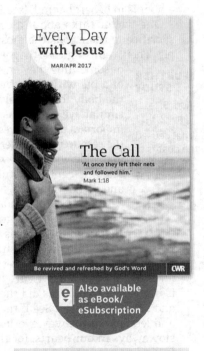

Every Day
with Jesus
MAR/APR 2017

The Call
'At once they left their nets and followed him.'
Mark 1:18

Be revived and refreshed by God's Word **CWR**

Also available as eBook/ eSubscription

Obtain your copy from CWR, a Christian bookshop or National Distributor.
If you would like to take out a subscription, see the order form at the back of these notes.

'Yes – No'

FOR READING & MEDITATION – PSALM 139:1–24

'See if there is any offensive way in me, and lead me in the way everlasting.' (v24)

Yesterday we touched on how it can be difficult, at times, to trust God. The old 'pharaoh' has been used to ruling you for decades, so when it is asked to release you from slavery and let you go into freedom it will say, 'Yes,' then just as easily say, 'No.' And then, 'Yes – No.' But you must insist, as did Moses, that 'not a hoof is to be left behind' (see Exod. 10:26).

One writer talks about a community that was about to sacrifice to their gods the most precious thing they had – a pig. Then, realising that they would be depriving themselves of something they enjoyed, decided to offer the head of a pig with the severed tail in its mouth, to keep the body for themselves. Many of us do something similar: we offer Jesus some things but keep the most important for ourselves. We offer our service and keep the resources. We offer our talents but retain the right to decide where and when we will use these talents. The self-centred nature remains, proud, imperious and demanding.

FURTHER STUDY

Acts 5:1–11;
Phil. 2:1–11

1. What caused the deaths of Ananias and Sapphira?

2. What was Jesus' example to us?

There is a custom among some North American Indians to give a gift and then take it back. It is called 'Indian giving'. This is so often what we do with God. We pass a resolution of 'full surrender' and then nullify it by adding riders. It does not necessarily mean we aren't sincere, for often our real motives are hidden from us. This is why it is important to pray, as did the psalmist, 'Search me, O God, and know my heart … See if there is any offensive way in me, and lead me in the way everlasting.' Let's do away with any stowaways in our hearts, for they will prevent Jesus having full sway. Mean what you say when you pray, and God will show you your true condition.

My Father, can You see any stowaways in my heart? If so, reveal them to me, for I would have done with anything that hinders Your life flowing through me. May everything be dedicated to You. Amen.

My *philia* becomes His *agape*

FOR READING & MEDITATION – 1 JOHN 4:7–21

'We love because he first loved us.' (v19)

As we learn to trust God and surrender to Him then the whole concept of loving ourselves takes on a different meaning. There is, as mentioned earlier, a natural love for self in the heart of each of us. It's a natural, healthy response to reach out to others, but if our love goes no further than ourselves then it is unhealthy and in danger of becoming stagnant. When we become Christians, receiving Jesus' love transforms the natural love with which we were born, and, in consequence, our love for others. Here is an illustration that shows this at work. A young girl whose appearance and character were beautiful wore on her neck a locket that no one was ever allowed to open. One day she confided to a friend that in the locket she carried something that governed the whole of her life. Her friend was allowed to open the locket and saw there these words: 'Whom having not seen ye love' (1 Pet. 1:8, KJV). She explained that all her life she had struggled with the problem of self. 'I had a natural love for myself,' she said, 'but I sensed it was tainted and imperfect and hence my love for others was tainted and imperfect. Then I received Jesus into my heart and I found that His love affected my love and turned my natural love into a love more and more like His.'

Does this make sense? Can you see that when we receive His perfect love, our love changes into the likeness of His own? A friend of mine says, 'My *philia* love [*philia* is the Greek word for human love] was changed to *agape* love [*agape* is the Greek word for divine love] simply by focusing on how much He loved me.' If you think you don't love Jesus enough, maybe you don't realise how much He loves you.

FURTHER STUDY

Deut. 7:6–9;
John 15:9–17

1. Why did God choose Israel?

2. Why did Jesus choose the disciples?

Father, I see that Your love flowing into my love turns my *philia* into Your *agape*. Let any scales that may still be on my eyes fall away so that I might see how much I am loved and learn to love as You do. In Jesus' name. Amen.

When ungodly thoughts persist

FOR READING & MEDITATION – MATTHEW 5:27–30

'But I tell you that anyone who looks at a woman lustfully has already committed adultery with her in his heart.' (v28)

The issue we turn to now in our pursuit of freedom in our lives is harmful and ungodly thoughts. In some people, all other troubles are minor in comparison with this. Time and time again I have talked with people who seemed calm and composed and presented as untroubled but who confessed that they were often plagued by wrong thoughts. Montaigne, the French essayist, spoke about people whose heads were 'a merry-go-round of lustful images'. Many men and women have described their problem with troublesome thoughts to me in similar terms.

FURTHER STUDY

Rom. 1:18–25;
Eph. 4:17–24

1. What does wrong thinking lead to?

2. What is the way of life we can have in Jesus?

Sometimes dark thoughts are darts of the devil, but more often than not they come from our carnal nature and rise spontaneously in the mind. One writer, when describing how lustful thoughts can surface in the mind, says, 'They can be triggered by simple things like a picture, a word, a story, an advertisement, a glance, an odour … almost anything can summon a wrong thought to the mind, and in a passionate nature it is soon hot with desire.'

One thing must be made clear: we cannot stop wrong thoughts coming into our mind but we can take steps to deal with them once they do arise. I am sure you have heard the saying, 'You can't stop birds flying into your hair but you can stop them nesting there.' Dark thoughts are never to be regarded as sin; they become sin only when we give in to them, when we adopt them, own them and nurture them. The type of person Jesus referred to in our text today commits adultery in his heart not when the thought arises but when he indulges it, humours it and allows it to establish a foothold. Can Jesus help us here? There is no one better, as we shall see.

Father, help me, I pray, to recognise all improper thoughts as soon as they arise. Help me stop wrong thoughts from mounting into problems. In Jesus' name. Amen.

Perfect peace

FOR READING & MEDITATION – ISAIAH 26:1–9

*'You will keep in perfect peace him whose mind is steadfast,
because he trusts in you.' (v3)*

The area of the mind that is most involved in the struggle with wrong thoughts is the imagination. In our text today the word 'mind' could be translated 'imagination'. The verse would then begin, 'You will keep in perfect peace him whose imagination stops at You.'

When an unhealthy thought arises in the mind we need not be ashamed. However, the way we deal with it at this stage is very important. Rather than allowing our imagination to take over, we *can* control it so that it stops at God and we take no further action. Take ungodly sexual thoughts, for example. If we allow an eager imagination to indulge itself and daydream about the idea instead of bringing it to God then, having lost the first round in the imagination, it is not surprising if the defeat results in us taking action.

Once I had a debate with someone who said that sexual desires are not a matter of the mind at all; they have a physical basis. But no sharp distinction can be drawn between mind and body. As Dr W.E. Sangster illustrated, 'The mind does not live within the body as a kernel exists within the shell of a nut. Mind and body are interwoven in a way not yet fully understood, but each reacts upon the other.' Whether or not a sexual thought arises from the physical is not the point; the mind soon takes over and it is here the struggle takes place. Life comes to us with strong motivations and instincts but God has shown us we are free to resist and give our thoughts to Him. We live lives in which biblical principles guide and direct us. This means we can live fully and freely, just as God originally intended.

FURTHER STUDY

2 Sam. 11:2–7, 14–17,26–27;
Matt. 15:10–20;
1 Thess. 4:1–8

1. How did King David displease the Lord?

2. What instructions did Paul give?

Father, I see how my imagination plays such a part in the battle of the mind. Help me to always be alert to this fact. So fill my imagination with truth and light that wrong thoughts shall find no place to thrive. In Jesus' name. Amen.

'The law of reversed effect'

FOR READING & MEDITATION – NEHEMIAH 4:15–23

'Our God will fight for us!' (v20)

A recent and very serious problem facing the Church at this time is the ease with which men and women can have access to unsuitable material on the internet. There is so much available just at the click of a button...

During a men's meeting – a very open, honest and non-judgmental meeting – I asked how many men had watched pornography online. To my concern, almost half of those present raised their hands. We began to pray together and there was a great moving of the Spirit in the hearts of these men. After the time of prayer, the discussion centred on how to live free from this problem, and I shared the way in which God has taught me to be free from ungodly thoughts. The advice I gave those men I now offer to you. Incidentally, although we have been talking mainly about sexual thoughts, these suggestions can be applied when other troublesome thoughts arise, for instance thoughts of envy, jealousy or spite.

FURTHER STUDY

Psa. 119:25–32;
Phil. 4:4–8

1. What does the psalmist hold fast to?

2. What is worth thinking about?

First, don't try to fight them in your own strength. Fighting (as we saw earlier) only seems to exacerbate the problem. You may have heard about the 'law of reversed effect', which results in a person achieving what they actually set out to avoid. Wrong thoughts are not driven out by dwelling on them, either guiltily or even prayerfully. It is an unhelpful tactic to direct sustained attention to wrong thoughts, even in an attitude of penitence or prayer. The longer they are the focus of attention, the deeper they are burned into the memory. Many Christians have lost the struggle with wrong thoughts because they hoped that by holding them in the mind and dwelling on them in prayer, the wrong thoughts would be dissolved. Sadly, not so.

Father, I long to walk in complete freedom in God. Save me from fastening on to ideas that may sound good and spiritual but are ineffective. To be at my best for You I need to follow the best principles. Help me dear Father. Amen.

FOR READING & MEDITATION – HEBREWS 12:1–11

'Let us fix our eyes on Jesus, the author and perfecter of our faith'
(v2)

If, as we saw yesterday, it is unhelpful and a waste of energy to direct sustained attention to wrong thoughts, even in an attitude of penitence or prayer, then how do we deal with them? Well, they can be outmanoeuvred by directing the mind to some other absorbing theme. The best one to turn our minds to is Jesus Himself. He is the centre of all things pure. Some years ago we used to sing a chorus that goes like this:

> *Turn your eyes upon Jesus,*
> *Look full in His wonderful face;*
> *And the things of earth will grow strangely dim*
> *In the light of His glory and grace.*

The following advice was given to me when I was a young Christian and I can vouch for its effectiveness. Whenever a wrong thought arises I turn my mind instantly to Jesus. I picture Him in the halls of my mind and I find that the thought that seemed so appealing before, and has had such a hold upon me, is now unappealing. I see it for what it is when I am conscious of the presence of Jesus. I have discovered that just to think of Him is to summon His aid.

It is positively amazing how passions are cooled and how serenity, rather than a gnawing sinful desire, is experienced when we turn the mind swiftly to Jesus. Christ in our heart and mind is a powerful safeguard. Romans 12:2 says, 'Do not conform any longer to the pattern of this world, but be transformed by the renewing of your mind.' We will look at how this process of transformation takes place in more detail tomorrow, but make it your prayer today that God will transform your mind so that you no longer waste your time with unhelpful, wrong thoughts.

FURTHER STUDY

1 Thess. 5:16–24;
Heb. 2:6–12

1. How does Paul instruct his readers and pray for them?

2. How does the writer of Hebrews see Jesus?

Father, this is what I long for when ungodly thoughts persist – coolness in place of heat; serenity instead of gnawing desire. Grant that as I put this principle into operation deliverance shall be my reward. In Jesus' name. Amen.

'May Jesus Christ be praised!'

FOR READING & MEDITATION – COLOSSIANS 3:1–17

'Let the word of Christ dwell in you richly' (v16)

The final suggestion I would like to make in finding freedom from wrong thoughts is this: in addition to turning your mind to Jesus, keep also in the ante-room of your mind certain good and beautiful thoughts to which you can direct your attention by a simple act of the will. These could include a passage of Scripture or a message you heard in a recent talk, but, let me stress, it is best if the thoughts are biblical. There is awesome power locked up in all scriptural truth, which *will* transform your mind. Learn to meditate on the Word of God and do what our text for today suggests: 'Let the word of Christ dwell in you richly'.

FURTHER STUDY

Psa. 1:1–6;
Matt. 7:24–29

1. How does the psalmist avoid the counsel of the wicked?

2. What contrasts the wise and the foolish man?

May I suggest that each time you come across a Scripture that strikes you with its power and beauty, meditate upon it. One of the best times to meditate is just before you go to sleep, as your last thought sinks into your subconscious and remains there through the night. Your subconscious mind goes on working while you are asleep, so let it work on Scripture! The more of God's Word you hold in your heart, the more readily available it will be for your mind to turn to when it is plagued by ungodly thoughts. Just as light dispels darkness, so the light of God's Word when introduced into the mind causes dark thoughts to flee.

We have spent the last month looking at ways in which we can walk into the freedom that Jesus has already won for us. My prayer is that you have already begun to walk in that freedom – and will continue to do so, perhaps using my suggestions as aids. Remember, the key is in submitting to God and trusting Him – His power and strength gives us everything we need to live life to the full.

Father, help me to have a heart that is focused on purity of thought and to build the strategies I have learned this month into my life. I ask this in and through the peerless and powerful name of Jesus. Amen.

Order form

4 Easy Ways To Order

1. Phone in your credit card order: **01252 784700** (Mon–Fri, 9.30am – 5pm)
2. Visit our online store at **www.cwr.org.uk/store**
3. Send this form together with your payment to: **CWR, Waverley Abbey House, Waverley Lane, Farnham, Surrey GU9 8EP**
4. Visit a Christian bookshop

For a list of our National Distributors, who supply countries outside the UK, visit **www.cwr.org.uk/distributors**

Your Details (required for orders and donations)

Full Name:	CWR ID No. (if known):
Home Address:	
	Postcode:
Telephone No. (for queries):	Email:

Publications

TITLE	QTY	PRICE	TOTAL
		Total Publications	
UK P&P: up to £24.99 = **£2.99**; £25.00 and over = **FREE**			
Elsewhere P&P: up to £10 = **£4.95**; £10.01 – £50 = **£6.95**; £50.01 – £99.99 = **£10**; £100 and over = **£30**			
Total Publications and P&P (please allow 14 days for delivery)		**A**	

All CWR adult Bible reading notes are also available in **eBook** and **email subscription** format. Visit **www.cwr.org.uk** for further information.

Subscriptions* (non direct debit)

	QTY	PRICE (including P&P)			TOTAL
		UK	Europe	Elsewhere	
Every Day with Jesus (1yr, 6 issues)		£15.95	£19.95		
Large Print *Every Day with Jesus* (1yr, 6 issues)		£15.95	£19.95	Please contact nearest National Distributor or CWR direct	
Inspiring Women Every Day (1yr, 6 issues)		£15.95	£19.95		
Life Every Day (Jeff Lucas) (1yr, 6 issues)		£15.95	£19.95		
Mettle: 15–18s (1yr, 3 issues)		£14.50	£16.60		
YP's: 11–14s (1yr, 6 issues)		£15.95	£19.95		
Topz: 7–11s (1yr, 6 issues)		£15.95	£19.95		
Cover to Cover Every Day		Email subscription only, to order visit online store.			
Total Subscriptions (subscription prices already include postage and packing)				**B**	

Please circle which issue you would like your subscription to commence from:

JAN/FEB MAR/APR MAY/JUN JUL/AUG SEP/OCT NOV/DEC   *Mettle* JAN–APR MAY–AUG SEP–DEC

*Only use this section for subscriptions paid for by credit/debit card or cheque. For Direct Debit subscriptions see overleaf.

We promise to never share your details with other charities. By giving us your personal information, you agree that we may use this to send you information about the ministry of CWR. If you do not want to receive further information by post, please tick here. ☐

Continued overleaf >>

Payment Details

☐ I enclose a cheque/PO made payable to CWR for the amount of: **£** _____

☐ Please charge my credit/debit card.

Cardholder's Name (in BLOCK CAPITALS) _____

Card No. ☐☐☐☐ ☐☐☐☐ ☐☐☐☐ ☐☐☐☐

Expires End ☐☐ ☐☐   Security Code ☐☐☐

Gift to CWR   ☐ Please send me an acknowledgement of my gift   **C** ☐

Gift Aid (your home address required, see overleaf)

giftaid it   I am a UK taxpayer and want CWR to reclaim the tax on all my donations for the four years prior to this year **and on** all donations I make from the date of this Gift Aid declaration until further notice.*

Taxpayer's Full Name (in BLOCK CAPITALS) _____

Signature _____   **Date** _____

* I am a UK taxpayer and understand that if I pay less Income Tax and/or Capital Gains Tax than the amount of Gift Aid claimed on all my donations in that tax year it is my responsibility to pay any difference.

GRAND TOTAL (Total of A, B & C)   ☐

Subscriptions by Direct Debit (UK bank account holders only)

One-year subscriptions cost £15.95 (except *Mettle*: £14.50) and include UK delivery. Please tick relevant boxes and fill in the form below.

☐ *Every Day with Jesus* (1yr, 6 issues)
☐ Large Print *Every Day with Jesus* (1yr, 6 issues)
☐ *Inspiring Women Every Day* (1yr, 6 issues)
☐ *Life Every Day* (Jeff Lucas) (1yr, 6 issues)

☐ *Mettle*: 15–18s (1yr, 3 issues)
☐ *YP's*: 11–14s (1yr, 6 issues)
☐ *Topz*: 7–11s (1yr, 6 issues)

Issue to commence from

☐ Jan/Feb ☐ Jul/Aug   *Mettle* ☐ Jan–Apr
☐ Mar/Apr ☐ Sep/Oct   ☐ May–Aug
☐ May/Jun ☐ Nov/Dec   ☐ Sep–Dec

CWR Instruction to your Bank or Building Society to pay by Direct Debit

DIRECT Debit

Please fill in the form and send to: CWR, Waverley Abbey House, Waverley Lane, Farnham, Surrey GU9 8EP

Name and full postal address of your Bank or Building Society

To: The Manager _____ Bank/Building Society

Address _____

_____

_____

Postcode _____

Name(s) of Account Holder(s)

_____

Branch Sort Code

☐☐ ☐☐ ☐☐

Bank/Building Society Account Number

☐☐☐☐☐☐☐☐

Originator's Identification Number

4	2	0	4	8	7

Reference

☐☐☐☐☐☐☐☐☐☐☐☐☐☐☐☐☐☐

Instruction to your Bank or Building Society

Please pay CWR Direct Debits from the account detailed in this Instruc subject to the safeguards assured by the Direct Debit Guarantee.
I understand that this Instruction may remain with CWR and, if so, deta will be passed electronically to my Bank/Building Society.

Signature(s)

_____

Date _____

Banks and Building Societies may not accept Direct Debit Instructions for some types of account